Hofmannsthal's Novel *Andreas*

BY DAVID H. MILES

Hofmannsthal's Novel

Andreas

MEMORY AND SELF

PRINCETON UNIVERSITY PRESS

PRINCETON, NEW JERSEY

1972

This book has been composed in Linotype Janson

Designed by Jan Lilly

Printed in the United States of America

by Princeton University Press,

Princeton, New Jersey

To Jennie

PREFACE

DESPITE the highly symbolic and complex nature of his writings—or perhaps directly because of it—Hofmannsthal has had to suffer more than most writers at the hands of systematizing critics. A standard view emerging from the criticism of the past generation is that his life and works constitute a well-made three-act play or, perhaps better, a series of three *tableaux vivants*. In the first *tableau* we see him as a Viennese prodigy and aesthete, composing delicate verse and lyrical dramas (*Der Tor und der Tod*). Part two presents him as the "committed" married man, producing dramas, moralities (*Jedermann*), opera libretti (*Der Rosenkavalier*), and ethical prose works (*Die Frau ohne Schatten*). The last act unveils him as master seer, as the supreme designer of subtle comedy and profound tragedy (*Der Schwierige* and *Der Turm*). This triadic scheme is not the only one that has been proposed. Other critics, for instance, have preferred to emphasize only the first two stages. Ignoring any misgivings they might have about the "intentional fallacy," they have turned to Hofmannsthal's own self-analyses for support and, reading *Ad me ipsum* as a cleverly disguised *Ad scholasticos omnes*, have sketched a portrait of the artist as moving, by way of the "language crisis" of the famous Chandos letter, from aestheticism to *littérature engagée*, from private poems to public performances, from static image to dynamic gesture, from "pre-existence" to "existence." Still other critics have perceived even finer gradations of development, of the order of magical, mystical, mystical-magical, and so on, within the first period alone. Yet in the end, no matter which of these schemes is selected, the result is all too often a reduction of the act of interpretation to one of mere classification.

The difficult truth is that Hofmannsthal, like most writers, even those as radically different as Brecht, was a complex *combination* of aesthete and moralist. The emphasis may vary, but the same root tension remains: poets simply do not progress from one stage to another. The complete aesthete, like the total moralist, would most likely not write books at all. The present study hopes to avoid all such "cheap antitheses of 'art' and 'life,'" as Hofmannsthal himself put it (A, 139), by the twofold method already indicated in its title and subtitle—namely, by the pluralistic investigation of one particular work and by the tracing through many works of one particular theme. Part I thus attempts to demonstrate a few of the widely differing meanings that the phenomenon of memory assumed for Hofmannsthal. Above all, memory furnished him with his concept of time. For unlike most twentieth-century writers Hofmannsthal conceived of human time, not as the antithesis of a dehumanized clock-time, but rather as a complicated dialectic of remembering and forgetting. This simple fact helps to explain and reconcile much in his works: his leanings toward such diverse doctrines as those of Neoplatonism, Freudianism, and Christianity, his thoughts on poetic creation and "pre-existence," his views on art and morals, and, not least of all, his attempts to bring present politics into contact once more with a deeper sense of cultural tradition.

Part II, then, emerging from the statements on memory and self in the Introduction and Part I, presents a detailed and comprehensive interpretation of Hofmannsthal's sole novel. Begun in 1907 and constituting an eighty-page fragment (plus fifty pages of notes) when the author died in 1929, the novel clearly stands in the tradition of the German Bildungsroman, and as such leads us directly to questions that occupied Hofmannsthal for his entire life—namely, those concerning the nature of human personality and the possibility of human growth. Moreover, in terms of its form, the novel presents a poetic statement by Hofmannsthal that is at once more subjective than his essays and yet more objective than his lyrics and dramas. On the level of literary history it is equally fascinating, for it is above all a Janus-faced work, pointing both forward to the psychological phantasies of twentieth-century fiction and back to the phantasmagoric adventures of German romantic literature. (Hofmannsthal, who set the novel in the eighteenth century, made extensive use, for instance, of a work by an American psychologist that also influenced Joyce's *Finnegans Wake*.) Thus, between its standard Bildungsroman plot and its modern spatial form, its traditional ideals and modern realities, the novel presents to the reader a fascinating combination of conflicting elements, both in literary history and in the writer himself.

The original impetus for this study, which began, in a rather different form, as a 1968 Ph.D. dissertation at Princeton University, was the discrepancy I sensed between the constant critical acclaim of *Andreas* and the lack of a single comprehensive study of the novel in either English or German. (Gautschi's dissertation was the first step in this direction.) Moreover, among the large number of studies of Hofmannsthal in German, most deal with his dramas, essays, and poetry; his prose fiction has received much less attention. Furthermore, and this is an additional reason for Part I of my study, despite the rising interest in Hofmannsthal in this country there are astoundingly few studies on him in English.

In view of the fact that we are still awaiting publication of the critical edition of Hofmannsthal's works, I have used the fifteen-volume edition put out by Fischer Verlag (see the page of abbreviations). For translations I have relied, where possible, on the three-volume Bollingen Series edition edited by Michael Hamburger: Hugo von Hofmannsthal, *Selected Prose* (which contains the complete *Andreas*, including the notes) (New York, 1952); *Poems and Verse Plays* (New York, 1961); *Selected Plays and Libretti* (New York, 1963). In some cases, however, either because of slight inaccuracies or for reasons of emphasis, I have altered the translations. A handy smaller edition of Hofmannsthal, also containing *Andreas*, is the two-volume one also published by Fischer Verlag: Hugo von Hofmannsthal, *Ausgewählte Werke in zwei Bänden*, ed. R. Hirsch (Frankfurt a. M., 1957). Margaret Jacobs' edition of *Andreas* in: Hugo von Hofmannsthal, *Four Stories* (Oxford, 1968), contains excellent notes.

As for secondary works, those I have made use of are cited in footnotes and listed in the index. In view of the immense growth of Hofmannsthal studies in recent years it seemed pointless to attempt a complete bibliography here. For those less familiar with Hofmannsthal, however, I would like to suggest the following brief list of works: in English, the three introductions to the Bollingen Series are excellent short pieces on Hofmannsthal; in German the best introduction is in A. Soergel/C. Hohoff, *Dichtung und Dichter der Zeit* (Düsseldorf, 1961), I, 448-494. Important collections of articles on Hofmannsthal are found in both Richard Alewyn, *Über Hugo von Hofmannsthal* (Göttingen, 1963), and *Hugo von Hofmannsthal—Wege der Forschung*, ed. S. Bauer (Darmstadt, 1968). (Both of these contain Alewyn's important article on *Andreas*.) Erwin Kobel,

Hugo von Hofmannsthal (Berlin, 1970), gives a general view of eighteen works of Hofmannsthal from a somewhat metaphysical standpoint, but does not include *Andreas*. The best single published work on *Andreas* is the Swiss dissertation by Karl Gautschi, *Hugo von Hofmannsthals Romanfragment 'Andreas'* (diss. Zürich, 1965). Werner Volke, *Hugo von Hofmannsthal* (Hamburg, 1967) is the only study we have that approaches a biography of the poet. Apart from the standard bibliography by Horst Weber (Berlin, 1966), covering the years 1892-1963, there are useful shorter bibliographies in both Volke and Gotthart Wunberg, *Der frühe Hofmannsthal* (Stuttgart, 1965).

During the various stages of its preparation my study has profited from the help and comments of a number of people. I am grateful to the University of Massachusetts for a research grant during the summer of 1969 and to the Alexander von Humboldt-Stiftung for a year's research fellowship to Germany during 1970-1971, when the major work on this study was completed. I would also like to thank Molly Matson for her constant and cheerful willingness to seek out necessary materials for me, and to Paul Leu I am grateful for stimulating discussions. Stanley Corngold, Ralph Freedman, and Alexander Gelley all gave the first draft of the book a careful yet sympathetic reading, and I am thankful for their comments. Richard Exner, whose intimate knowledge of Hofmannsthal made him an ideal reader of the manuscript, read all drafts and made invaluable suggestions. Finally, I would like to express a very special debt of thanks to Theodore Ziolkowski, whose criticism and advice were a constant help and whose encouragement was a gratifying support during the writing of the book.

At Princeton University Press I am particularly grateful to Marjorie Sherwood for her experienced eye in matters of style, and to R. Miriam Brokaw, Associate Director, for her interest in and enthusiasm about the project from the very beginning.

Last of all, I would like to thank my very first reader, my constant critic, typist, and domestic muse—to whom this book is dedicated.

DAVID H. MILES

Freiburg, Germany
May 1971

Abbreviations

I HAVE quoted from the following edition of Hofmannsthal's works: Hugo von Hofmannsthal. *Gesammelte Werke in Einzelausgaben*, ed. Herbert Steiner. 15 vols. Stockholm/Frankfurt am Main: S. Fischer Verlag, 1945-1959.

As the pagination in the different printings of this edition varies, it is important to note the year of each individual volume.

Die Erzählungen (1953)	E
Gedichte und Lyrische Dramen (1963)	G
Lustspiele I (1959)	LI
Lustspiele II (1965)	LII
Lustspiele III (1968)	LIII
Lustspiele IV (1956)	LIV
Prosa I (1956)	PI
Prosa II (1959)	PII
Prosa III (1964)	PIII
Prosa IV (1966)	PIV
Dramen I (1964)	DI
Dramen II (1966)	DII
Dramen III (1969)	DIII
Dramen IV (1958)	DIV
Aufzeichnungen (1959)	A
Briefe 1890–1901. Berlin, 1935	BI
Briefe 1900–1909. Vienna, 1937	BII

Contents

CONTENTS

INTRODUCTION

Time, Memory, and Self in the Bildungsroman

> The power of the memory is great, O Lord. It is awe-inspiring in its profound and incalculable complexity. Yet it is my mind: it is my self. What, then, am I, my God?
> Augustine, *Confessions*, (X, 17)

HE German Bildungsroman,[1] as Thomas Mann reminds us in his reflections on the *Zauberberg*, represents in a sense the mere "sublimation and spiritualization of the *Abenteurerroman*,"[2] the novel of adventure. Goethe makes much the same point in *Wilhelm Meister*, where he associates the novel with such English novels of adventure as *The Vicar of Wakefield* and *Tom Jones*,[3] in which a variety of colorful episodes is allowed to pass in front of the reader's eyes. In general, German critics have adhered to this view as well, discovering the antecedents of the Bildungsroman in either such medieval epics as *Parzival* or in picaresque novels such as Grimmelshausen's *Simplicissimus*. The hero of the Bildungsroman, in other words, is regarded as a distant descendant of the quester hero of the Middle Ages, a sort of picaro

[1] I have not attempted to translate *Bildungsroman* in this study. Although there do exist "novels of education" in English—*David Copperfield*, *Sons and Lovers*, and *A Portrait of the Artist as a Young Man* are all good examples—the German term has found no ready equivalent in English.

[2] "Einführung in den 'Zauberberg,'" in *Der Zauberberg* (Frankfurt a. M., 1959), p. xv (translated into English as "The Making of *The Magic Mountain*").

[3] J. W. Goethe, *Werke*, ed. Erich Trunz (Hamburg, 1965), VII, 307.

in search of the bourgeois values of profession, marriage, and a sense of identity. For like the picaro he is a highly undramatic creation, essentially a passive reflector of epic experience (with the difference, of course, that the picaro does not develop). The hero, in short, must proceed with the ambling direction of a Tom Jones; he must, as Goethe puts it, become a passive, accumulating center for experience, a man of "events" rather than "deeds."[4]

A second narrative characteristic the Bildungsroman has in common with both the adventure novel and the picaresque is the device of the journey: the Bildungsroman traditionally rests on the institution of the *Bildungsreise*, the odyssey in which the self is sought in other lands and among other peoples. The journey assures the variety of experience necessary to true growth and at the same time provides a narrative framework that also carries important implications for the time-structure of the novel. The standard time-pattern of the Bildungsroman is chronological, a fact that relates it to both the biography and the adventure novel but that also distinguishes it sharply from such forms as the psychological novel, with its complex levels of subjective, *non*-chronological time, and from more objective forms such as that of the sociological novel, with its more condensed span of time and more panoramic unfolding of episodes in space.

The parallels to the picaresque novel, the fact of the passive hero, and the chronological pattern of the journey all belong to the standard view of the Bildungsroman, one that has already been discussed—and debated—by many

---

[4] Goethe's emphasis on the passive, unheroic quality of the protagonist—Wilhelm being by no means a *Meister*—not only points to the importance of the critical, ironic strain in the Bildungsroman (as in the *Zauberberg*) but also forecasts the advent of the modern antihero: Wilhelm, in a sense, is the first "Mann ohne Eigenschaften."

critics.[5] I would like to suggest, however, that there exists yet another fictional forerunner and component of the Bildungsroman that is equally as important as that of the unilinear quest and that, to my knowledge, has been overlooked by criticism to date. This is the narrative pattern of the spiritual autobiography or confession. Representing in a sense the mere inversion of picaresque materials, a form of *inner* journey, the literary confession shares with the Bildungsroman both its will to educate and, even more important, its concern for the psychological problem and possibility of human growth and change. Styling itself precisely as a moral antidote to the scandalous chronicles of the adventure novel, the confession replaces the picaro's love of adventure for adventure's sake with a plea for reflection and reform. Rousseau, for instance, on the very first page of his *Confessions*, admits that the reader may well groan at the depravities and misdeeds that are to follow but insists that before passing judgment the reader turn inward and examine his own soul as well.

The importance of recognizing the literary confession, as well as the adventure-novel, as a forerunner of the Bildungsroman is that it makes us aware of an entirely different concept of Bildung and, consequently, of narrative structure as well. This difference in attitude toward Bildung can perhaps best be illustrated by quoting from two typical Bildungsromane, the first belonging more to the adventure type, the second to the confessional. "From youth onward," one earnest hero assures us, "my subconscious wish has been the cultivation of my individual self, just as I am." In a second novel, however, we are confronted with a situation radically different: "It seemed to him after some reflection that his self had disappeared—and that he would have

---

[5] See Lothar Köhn's excellent *Forschungsbericht, Entwicklungs- und Bildungsroman* (Stuttgart, 1969).

to search for it again in the series of his memories of the past. Indeed, he felt that the very existence of the self depended on an unbroken chain of such memories."[6] The obvious difference here is that for the first hero the unity of personality is an assumed fact, and growth thus means above all the act of experiencing life itself. For the second, however, the self is no longer simply a *donnée*, but must first be sought among the innumerable shards of memory; growth here means reflection. The hero's motto might be the existentialized Cartesian formula: "I remember, therefore I am."

This discovery that Bildung depends upon memory—that a healthy sense of self is based not upon experience itself but rather upon remembered, reordered experience—is not, however, necessarily a discovery made in the cork-lined room of a Proust or on the couch of the analyst, much as this idea may recall the insights of modern psychology. Not only does our second quotation come from a novel of the eighteenth century (one typically subtitled "A Psychological Novel"), but one of the very earliest classics of Western literature, the *Confessions* of St. Augustine, also presents us with the same insight. The self, for Augustine, is above all a phenomenon of memory: memory "*is* my self," he states, for "without it I could not even speak of myself." For Augustine the phenomenon of time itself is also a function of memory: the past, he writes, is nothing but "a long remembrance of the past."[7] In short, the *Confessions*, despite their framework of Christian and Neoplatonic transcendence, present us with an early example of a deeply psychological Bildungsroman of the confessional order.

[6] Goethe, *Werke*, VII, 290; Karl Philipp Moritz, *Anton Reiser* (Munich, 1961), p. 201.

[7] *Confessions*, trans. R. S. Pine-Coffin (Baltimore, 1966), pp. 223 (my italics), and 277.

The confessional mode of fiction, with its different concept of personality structure, often brings with it a different narrative structure as well, one that relates it directly to the psychological novel. Precisely because the meditative quest is an inner one, as opposed to the outer events of the *Bildungsreise*, it need not and often does not adhere to the fiction of clock- and calendar-time. This fact is best described by the thoughts of a reflective hero in a modern Bildungsroman: suddenly "it occurred to him that that order of life for which one yearns, overburdened as one is, and dreaming of simplicity, is none other than that of narrative order! That simple order that consists in being able to say: 'When that had happened, then this happened!' What puts our mind at rest is the simple sequence, the overwhelming variegation of life now represented in . . . a unidimensional order."[8] The fact is that for the reflective or confessional hero, life can never adhere to the comforting sequence of chronological narrative order, with its consoling illusion of progress and causality. Although most people would like to imagine it thus, this "primitive epic element"[9] has little to do with real life. The narrative order which is left for the meditative hero is in fact a non-order: scattered entries in notebooks, collections of essayistic fragments, or confessional jottings in a private diary. The calendar chronology of real episodes (this and then that happened) gives way to the private chronology of the psyche, whereby form is dictated by the polydimensional mirror of memory.

Yet the two basic modes of the epic quest and the retrospective confession are obviously not mutually exclusive. Although it is indeed useful to be able to speak of them separately—as is the case with all generic concepts in criticism

---

[8] Robert Musil, *Der Mann ohne Eigenschaften* (Hamburg, 1970), p. 650.
[9] *Ibid.*

—the two can and often do combine in actual literary works. Indeed, this is quite apparent in the novel that founded the tradition of the Bildungsroman, *Wilhelm Meister*. The first five books of the work, centering on Wilhelm's associations with a troupe of traveling actors, are largely picaresque; the sixth book, the "Confessions of a Beautiful Soul," is composed of reflective, introspective elements; and the last two books of the novel, concentrating on the projects of the symbolic Tower Society, effectively combine the two levels, allowing the plane of adventure to merge with the plane of reflection. In its most general shape then, the novel presents a dialectic of Bildung, or, to phrase it more in the language of Goethe, a progression through a diastole and a systole to a higher, rhythmic resolution of the two. Whereas the band of actors is less than "gebildet," and the pietistic aunt of the confessions is in fact "überbildet,"[10] the Tower humanists present the ideal synthesis; they are active as well as reflective.

Once we have recognized that the adventure and confessional modes are tendencies rather than typological absolutes—and the same could also be demonstrated using novels other than *Wilhelm Meister*—an extremely interesting historical development becomes apparent. From *Wilhelm Meister* onward, the history of the Bildungsroman is one of an increasing movement *away* from the adventure mode, with its "primitive epic element," toward the multilayered forms of confessional narration—a movement away from the Goethean ideal of the entelechial, organic self toward one of the self as a "retrospective hypothesis," as Samuel Beckett has described it.[11] This progressive loss of the self, as it has also been called, by no means signals the demise of the Bildungsroman, but merely points to a new con-

[10] Goethe, *Werke*, VII, 518.   [11] *Proust* (New York, 1931), p. 4.

ception of Bildung. Beginning as a secondary assumption in various early "confessional" writers such as St. Augustine and Rousseau, existing as a tacit implication in both the theories of irony and the portraits of the *Doppelgänger* among the romantics, and finally gaining its widest currency through the theories of Freud and Jung on the "latent" and "shadow" selves residing in the unconscious, the idea that the self is in actuality many selves—ranging from the private to the mythic—has become a commonplace in modern literature. It reaches its ultimate perhaps in Musil's hero Ulrich, who possesses so many actual and possible dimensions of personality that he is quite literally a "man without a self."

The history of this phenomenon, the journey away from the Goethean model of Bildung, could easily be traced in the development of the Bildungsroman during the nineteenth and early twentieth centuries. Structurally, it is signalled by the increasing use of the multilayered forms of essayism, the flashback, and the diary. Whereas in *Wilhelm Meister*, for instance, the confessional elements are entirely subordinated to the epic flow of events, in a modern work such as Rilke's *Die Aufzeichnungen des Malte Laurids Brigge*, which in many ways represents the most consistent and extreme example in the development of the confessional Bildungsroman, the structure is precisely the reverse: the hero's *Bildungsreise* recedes to a mere background motif while his reflections and confessions move to the center of the narrative to become the guiding structural force. Thematically, this historical development converges with the increasing emphasis on the importance of childhood memories; such phrases as "the feeling had come over me that I actually hadn't experienced a youth," "childhood days that are still unexplained," and "to die reconciled with his

9

childhood,"[12] would be inconceivable as expressions of the Goethean concept of Bildung as presented in *Wilhelm Meister*.

The last quotation is from *Andreas*, and Hofmannsthal's position in this development is a highly significant one. Of all modern German writers, Hofmannsthal probably experienced most deeply and tragically the rift between the world of German classicism and that of the twentieth century. *Andreas* represents, among other things, the impossible attempt to fuse the modern sensibility of a Rilke or a Kafka with the ideals and outlook of a Goethe. As I attempt to demonstrate in the second part of this study, Hofmannsthal himself was torn between what Hermann Broch has termed the modes of self-confession and self-suppression; and the novel, with its epic beginning and open, fragmentary "ending," mirrors this very same tension. Furthermore, Hofmannsthal's hero suffers from a similar conflict: almost half the novel amounts to a form of self-confession on the part of Andreas. Very much like such modern "heroes" as Rilke's Malte, he is a protagonist overburdened with memories and yet lacking a self. He is perhaps best understood against the background of the poet's earlier writings, against the themes of remembering and forgetting, and above all against the figures of the Neoplatonic poet and the aesthetic adventurer.

[12] Gottfried Keller, *Der grüne Heinrich* in *Sämtliche Werke und ausgewählte Briefe* (Munich, 1963), I, 951; Rainer Maria Rilke, *Die Aufzeichnungen des Malte Laurids Brigge* in *Sämtliche Werke* (Frankfurt a. M., 1966), VI, 724; *Andreas* (E,222).

PART I The Past, The Poet, and the
Route to Bildung

ONE   The Neoplatonic Looking-Glass:

The Past as Escape

> He would need then, to grow accustomed to the sight of that upper world. At first it would be easiest to make out shadows, and then images of men and things reflected in water, and later the things themselves. . . . Last of all, he would be able to look at the Sun and contemplate its nature, not as it appears when reflected in water . . . but as it is . . . in its own domain.
>
> Plato, The Parable of the Cave

*N*owadays," Hofmannsthal wrote in 1893, "two things appear to be modern: the analysis of life and the flight from life. . . . Reflection or fantasy, mirror-image or dream-image. Young nerves and old furniture have become modern" (PI, 149). As the nineteen-year-old Hofmannsthal was quick to assess, the prevailing intellectual attitudes in Europe at the turn of the century were indeed sharply divided. Like the hero of a Schnitzler drama, Europe, and particularly Hofmannsthal's Vienna, was caught between the naturalistic urge to analyze itself and the impressionistic impulse to lose itself in the dream-like flux of the present: positivism and symbolism, naturalism and neo-romanticism, Freud and Mallarmé were the ruling fashions of the day. As Hofmannsthal puts it in the same essay, two basic drives overshadowed the current morality: "the drive to understand and that to forget" (PI, 150).

Hofmannsthal's analysis of the intellectual climate, however, applies even more to the poet himself, for he conceived of his own art, of the poetic image in particular, as arising at precisely that point where the world

13

without—the world of the mirror—impinged upon the world within—that of the dream. Existing on the borderline between sight and insight, the real and the symbolic, the immanent and the transcendent, Hofmannsthal's Image informs his entire aesthetic, particularly during the years of his so-called lyric decade, from 1890 to 1900. The key to this conjunction of two worlds in one image lies above all in the phenomenon of memory. Again and again Hofmannsthal likens memory to a world that is of reality and yet also somehow beyond it, much like the reality of dreams. Thus he likens the memory of a trip he had taken to Provence with his tutor following graduation from Gymnasium to the reality of a Chinese picture-book, to the reality of images in dreams; for the memories are "as strange as if they hadn't been real" (PI, 77). The sudden recollection of a spring day in the middle of winter could arouse a similar feeling in the poet: "The snow-covered Schwarzenberg garden, with its shadowy memories of May afternoons, expressed most vividly this great enigma of life, that all things live for themselves and yet are full of connections with one another" (A, 117); elsewhere, speaking of "advancing toward pure vision," he mentions how in winter "the frost-patterns of flowers on a window pane can suddenly flood the soul with the happy feeling of midsummer" (PIII, 169-170). In each instance the memories evoke within the poet the mysterious sense of a deep, all-pervading unity in the world, between things seen and unseen.

This impact that remembered experience had upon the early Hofmannsthal—memory's double quality of mirror *and* dream—actually relates him to the Neoplatonic tradition and its theories of both time and memory. For Neoplatonism, which traditionally views the tangible world as a mere image or reflection of the higher realm of the eternal ideas, makes memory an important link between these two realms. According to the doctrine of anamnesis or recollection put forth in Plato's *Phaedo* and the *Meno*, one "knows" the higher world through a process of re-cognition on the part of the soul. Thus Socrates, in the *Meno*, is able to elicit higher geometrical reasoning from a lowly slave boy simply by "refreshing" his memory. Many poets besides Hofmannsthal have, of course, been strongly influenced by the Neoplatonic tradition, perhaps because the very vividness of the recollected images—particularly for the lyric poet— lends them a "timeless," preternatural aspect. Wordsworth, for instance, in recognizing that the most sublime flights of the poetic imagination originate in "emotion recollected in tranquillity," and that we similarly draw our "intimations of immortality from recollections of early childhood," is actually saying much the same thing as does Hofmannsthal when he proclaims through one of his dramatic characters that "it is memory that makes us gods" (DI, 451). The experience was obviously autobiographical in part, for Hofmannsthal's own memory, as his friend Carl J. Burckhardt tells us, "was totally unique." In fact, his relationship to time was "entirely different from the normal one and this not in a speculative, but in a transcendent sense. . . . His knowledge and perception were, in the Platonic sense, a form of recollection."[1]

This Neoplatonic trait in Hofmannsthal's early view of memory is most strikingly evident in his attitude toward beauty. For his experience of all that was beautiful, as he explains in an essay, was "as if I were only remembering something much earlier" (PIII, 170).[1a] Indeed, because of his strong—almost eidetic—susceptibility to recollected images, Hofmannsthal also felt many of his most intense

---

[1] Carl J. Burckhardt, "Erinnerung an Hofmannsthal," in *Hugo von Hofmannsthal: Der Dichter im Spiegel der Freunde*, ed. H. Fiechtner (Bern, 1963), p. 130. [1a] Cf. Plato's *Phaedrus*, 251.

15

experiences to be mere semblances of some unknown experience in the past. Like the hero in Yeats's poem "He Remembers Forgotten Beauty," he senses, when he discovers beauty, not the splendor of the moment, but rather the faint reminder of a loveliness long since faded from the world. In the lyrical prose sketch "Das Glück am Weg," for instance, the poet catches a glimpse of a beautiful girl on a passing ship and describes the encounter as follows: "In that moment I knew two things: that she was very beautiful, and that I knew her, but from where? There arose within me something undefined, sweet, lovely, and past" (PI, 124). In the later essay "Augenblicke in Griechenland" the traveler describes his spiritual experience with the statues of the Athenian priestesses in the Acropolis Museum in words that are very similar, for he finds himself "remembering" their Apollonian beauty (PIII, 40). And in *Andreas* the same strange intuition assaults the hero in the scene where he first meets Sacramozo, his spiritual mentor in the novel. "Have I seen him before? How else could his image have made such a deep impression on me in one moment? I can learn about him from my own inner self!" (E, 174).

This sensation of paramnesia or *déjà vu*—the illusion that the present is but the repetition of some event lost in the past—is an aspect of the Neoplatonic tradition that, as Georges Poulet has pointed out, is particularly prominent in romantic thought.[2] Not only does this experience thus relate Hofmannsthal typologically to other poets—to Goethe, Novalis, and Yeats, for example[3]—but it also helps to clarify

[2] See Georges Poulet on "Timelessness and Romanticism," in *Journal of the History of Ideas*, 15 (1954), 3-22.

[3] In Goethe, for instance, see the lines in his poem "Warum gabst du uns die tiefen Blicke . . .": ". . . du warst in abgelebten Zeiten/ Meine Schwester oder meine Frau." There are countless examples in Novalis' *Heinrich von Ofterdingen*, as for instance at the end of the

Hofmannsthal's well-known concept of "pre-existence." The term of course derives from *Ad me ipsum*,[4] the self-interpretive jottings that Hofmannsthal began at the age of forty-two and that were published following his death. Not only is the general vocabulary of these notes strongly colored by Neoplatonism, but their very epigraph is taken from Gregory of Nyssa, one of the early Neoplatonic thinkers. The quotation characteristically appends to the basic Neoplatonic concept of the *Urbild* a touch of Christian millennialism: "He, the lover of the highest beauty, believed what he had already seen to be only the faint copy of what he had not yet seen, and desired to enjoy the original itself" (A, 213-214). Pre-existence, then, which Hofmannsthal mentions many times in *Ad me ipsum*,[5] is merely a private version of several common notions: on a philosophical level

---

eighth chapter where Mathilde says to Heinrich: "I feel I have known you since time immemorial." In Novalis, however, it should be noted that the phenomenon is not only psychological but metaphysical as well: the *déjà vu* also asserts the fundamental unity of self with world. For the parallels to Yeats, see Michael Hamburger's "Introduction" to the *Poems and Verse Plays* of Hofmannsthal (New York, 1961), pp. xliii-xlv. For a treatment of the general relationship between Neoplatonism and romanticism, see P. F. Reiff, "Plotin und die deutsche Romantik," *Euphorion*, 19 (1912), 591-612, as well as H-J. Mähl, "Novalis und Plotin," in *Jahrbuch des Freien Deutschen Hochstifts* (Tübingen, 1963), pp. 139-250, and M. H. Abrams, *Natural Supernaturalism* (New York, 1971), pp. 183-186.

[4] Ultimately, Hofmannsthal may have had the phrase from Pater, who mentions the Platonic idea of "pre-existence" in his essay on Winckelmann in *The Renaissance*, a book Hofmannsthal reviewed at the age of twenty. Pater also mentions "Plato's ante-natal state" in the essay on Michelangelo. Again, in his essay on Wordsworth in *Appreciations* (1889), Pater comments on the "mysterious notion of an earlier state of existence—the fancy of the Platonists—the old heresy of origin." Erwin Kobel, on the other hand, suggests in his study *Hugo von Hofmannsthal* (Berlin, 1970), p. 360, that the phrase may derive from Hofmannsthal's later readings of Kierkegaard. (See n. 77 below.)

[5] (A, 213-217, 220, 225-226, 230, 238, 242.)

17

it relates to the Platonic doctrine of the anamnesis of the soul; on a mythological level, to the romantic notion of a Golden Age during the childhood of the world; in psychological terms, to what Freud referred to in *Civilization and its Discontents* as the "oceanic feeling" of mystics, the regression to the limitless and unifying narcissism of the child (a process obviously capable of incorporating the sensation of paramnesia or *déjà vu* as well); and, on a theological level, it represents our private view of Eden before the Fall. It must be stressed, however, that for Hofmannsthal himself the concept of pre-existence belonged by and large to the private realm of aesthetic experience, particularly that of his youth, and not to any specific literary or philosophic tradition. In fact, in *Ad me ipsum*, he comments at one point that his feeling that "all beauty that is present in nature only seemed to point to something in the completely inaccessible past" was an "experience in youth (approximately from sixteen to twenty-two)" (A, 227).

The most misleading aspect of invoking the term pre-existence as a tool in Hofmannsthal criticism is that it can easily lead to a totally platonized Hofmannsthal, one in whom the bright edges of reality are blurred by shadowy assertions of the poet's belief in some ultimate unity lying totally beyond the realm of the seen. One of the most unusual and characteristic aspects of Hofmannsthal's Neoplatonic view of memory is that it is essentially anti-Platonic. Whereas traditional Platonism regards the recollected image as but a faded copy of the original divine idea and thus as a spiritual reflector of man's sacred origins, Hofmannsthal continually stresses the concrete immanence of the recollection, its focus on experiences in the real past. Unlike such Neoplatonists as Plotinus, who saw the soul as being dreadfully "befouled by its housing" and who was furthermore quite "ashamed to be in a body,"

Hofmannsthal was able to take pleasure in the sensuous as well as in the spiritual beauty of the world. In one of his early essays, in fact, he ridicules the typical fallacy of the Platonic artist who, in Lessing's well-known phrase, wants to become a "Raphael without hands" (PI, 31). In Hofmannsthal's eyes, poets may indeed be latent Platonists —for they, like children, are aware of the "heart of things," sensing in fish "the fish-ness, in gold the essence of gold" (PI, 276)—but nature for them, in the last analysis, always remains concrete and tangible. What other poets have described as the "memory of the golden forms," the "ghostly paradigm of things,"[6] bears little relevance to Hofmannsthal's poetic thought. Memory, instead of providing him in standard Platonic fashion with a pass from time to eternity, affords him the paradoxical experience of an *immanent* transcendence, as exemplified in the essay on Greece, where the statues, the virtual "bearers of eternity," exhibit at the same time a "breathtaking sensual presence" (PIII, 41, 38). Whereas Plato viewed time as the moving image of eternity, Hofmannsthal paradoxically brings eternity into time itself;[7] in his own words, he becomes a secular seer, a "mystic without mysticism" (A, 215).

Hofmannsthal's dual vision of the remembered image, then—as realistic mirror-image and as transcendent dream-image—represents basically an empiricized or psychologized version of the Neoplatonic view of memory. Although it would undoubtedly be rewarding to trace this neo-romantic view of the recollected image back through the symbolist image to the romantic cipher with its numinous, Neoplatonic overtones, as well as forward to the abso-

---

[6] Wallace Stevens, "Esthétique du Mal"; W. B. Yeats, "Among Schoolchildren."

[7] Here again Hofmannsthal is extremely close to what Poulet describes as one of the characteristic phenomena of romanticism. See "Timelessness and Romanticism," p. 7.

lute, autotelic images of expressionism,[8] the more interesting problem from our point of view is the question of precisely what images Hofmannsthal actually employed. For during his lyric decade in particular, Hofmannsthal made constant use of certain images to designate the poetic realm of memory itself, with its mirror-like dream of immanent transcendence.

Hofmannsthal's favorite metaphor for this realm is one of light, particularly reflected light, be this in a mirror, a body of water (as in a pond or a well), or even in the human eye itself. Thus in *Der weisse Fächer*, when Fortunio reflects on the past he sees it rise "as if from a deep, dark mirror" (G, 232), and the *Zurückgekehrter*, in his very first letter, refers to the "mirror of memory." Similarly Hofmannsthal, in the late essay on "Erinnerung," describes figures from the past as "detached mirror-images" and the poet in the "Vorspiel für ein Puppentheater" suddenly senses his former days emerging around him "like shadows from green mirrors." The image of the mirror-like surface of a pond or well serves the same purpose, signalling a shift to that magic realm of poetic consciousness that is present and yet somehow transcends the present. The most striking instance of this occurs in the poem "Weltgeheimnis," in which the deep, darkly mirroring surface of a well becomes Hofmannsthal's symbol for the magic looking-glass of the poet, the lover, and the child:

> Auf dessen dunklen Spiegel bückt
> Sich einst ein Kind und wird entrückt.   (G, 15)

One might be reminded here of the image of the deep "well of the past" that Thomas Mann mentions at the opening of the *Josephsromane*, and yet the differences between the two

---

[8] This progressive "secularization" of the Platonic image has been touched upon by both Frank Kermode in *Romantic Image* (New York, 1964), and August Closs in "The Shattered Image," *The Aryan Path* (Bombay, India), 36 (1965), 290-295, 337-342, 405-409.

images explain Hofmannsthal's intentions better than do the similarities: whereas Mann is primarily concerned with experiences of a mythic, archetypal cast, Hofmannsthal is speaking of a mode of experience inescapably personal and private, and limited to certain magic moments in time. Thus the young man in *Das kleine Welttheater* suddenly has the strange feeling that he has seen his white-haired father below him "in a well" (G, 304), and in an essay the poet-narrator suddenly glimpses his childhood "in the distance like a deep mountain lake" and proceeds to step into it "as if it were a house" (PII, 352). In each case the reflecting surface signals the private entrance to the dream-like world of memory.[9]

The images of the mirror, the pond, and the well easily connect with the idea of the human eye itself as a reflector; this image in particular becomes one of Hofmannsthal's most subtle for expressing that strange presentness of the past that is sensed in moments of heightened poetic consciousness. In *Das kleine Welttheater*, for instance, the poet sees the lakes and ponds as the virtual eyes of the landscape. The experience occurs at dusk—the time at which, as Hofmannsthal himself pointed out, lakes appear to hold

[9] This motif may also be connected with Hofmannsthal's memories of the wells and springs in the Alpine villages of the Salzkammergut, the resort area in Upper Austria where he spent most of his holidays since early childhood. In a letter to Burckhardt on August 24, 1924, for instance, Hofmannsthal actually comments at the age of fifty on the fact that he had been returning to the mountain springs of Fusch and drinking from their waters since he was ten years old. (Hugo von Hofmannsthal—Carl J. Burckhardt *Briefwechsel* [Frankfurt a. M., 1966], p. 158.) On the fact that the mirror in Hofmannsthal, as the symbolic entrance to an imaginary room, can become a "Transzendenz-Symbol," see Günther Erken, *Hofmannsthals dramatischer Stil* (Tübingen, 1967), p. 79. In general, Erken's whole chapter on "Spiegelung" in Hofmannsthal is excellent, although he concentrates largely on mirroring as a dramaturgical (and thus also metaphorical) principle, and stresses neither the mirror's Neoplatonic aspect nor its connection with creative recollection.

the light of day much longer than the surrounding landscape:[10]

> Nun setz ich mich am Rand des Waldes hin,
> Wo kleine Weiher lange noch den Glanz
> Des Tages halten und mit feuchtem Funkeln
> Die offnen Augen dieser Landschaft scheinen.
>
> (G, 300)

The image of the eye opening on a limitless past is an extremely common one in the early Hofmannsthal. In the poem "Kleine Erinnerungen" the poet discovers in the wide-open eyes of the "small sister" visions of a forgotten paradise; in "Dein Antlitz" the poet's memories of a formerly beloved valley are stirred by the light in his loved one's eyes. Moreover, in "Melusine" the nymph recalls her long-forgotten underwater paradise through the device of a double reflection: her memories are those of the outside world as it was once reflected in her own underwater eyes.

The figure of the poet himself, possessing the gift of "reflecting" the hidden past, figures prominently in the early works, his "magic" eye often leading to the comparison with a magician. Goethe's eye, for example, "must have been more mysterious than Klingsor's, the magician, more uncanny than Merlin's, whose eyes are said to have led down into the depths of hell like a bottomless pit" (PII, 45). And in the poem "Ein Traum von grosser Magie" the theme of the poet as magician is masterfully combined with the related motifs of recollection, dream, and reflecting eye:

> In seinen Augen aber war die Ruh
> Von schlafend- doch lebendgen Edelsteinen.
> Er setzte sich und sprach ein solches Du

---

[10] Burckhardt, "Erinnerung an Hofmannsthal," p. 143; also (A, 229).

Zu Tagen, die uns ganz vergangen scheinen,
Dass sie herkamen trauervoll und gross:
Das freute ihn zu lachen und zu weinen.

Er fühlte traumhaft aller Menschen Los. . . .

(G, 21)

The poet, for Hofmannsthal (in a formulation that anticipates Freud), is one who brings back the past through creative recollection, one who daydreams with open eyes.

A final, and perhaps the most striking, image that Hofmannsthal uses to express the poetic gift of reliving the past
in the present is that of starlight. The connection between
well and star, much like Hofmannsthal's observation on
ponds "collecting" light at dusk, is more than a trick of symbolist metaphor; it is based at least in part upon a concrete
fact of experience. As Hofmannsthal himself points out, if
we descend far enough into the shaft of a well by day, we
may actually catch sight of the stars above our head
(PIII, 117) (an experience of mystical union that, incidentally, also appealed to Rilke).[11] The great appeal of the
image of starlight for Hofmannsthal was largely due to the
fact that it could signify, by virtue of its space-time, the recollection of a long-lost past. In a diary entry of 1892 he
mentions the "speed of light: the star on which one can just
now watch the banquet of [the Roman emperor] Heliogaba-
lus taking place" (A, 97), and three years later he writes to
his friend Edgar Karg von Bebenburg, "There are stars
where light waves are now arriving that once emanated
from the spear with which a Roman soldier pierced the side
of our Savior; for that star, the event is now present."[12] Starlight thus becomes, in effect, a symbol of the miraculous
process whereby eternity may converge with time. As he

[11] See R. M. Rilke, *Briefe, 1907-1914* (Leipzig, 1933), p. 154.
[12] Letter of August 22, 1895; see also (A, 122).

puts it in a note in the *Buch der Freunde*: "There must be a star where things that happened a year ago are present, another where events of one hundred years ago are present, another for the time of the Crusades, and so on, everything in an uninterrupted chain; thus, in the eyes of eternity, everything exists next to one another in space" (A, 40). In short, the space-time of starlight becomes Hofmannsthal's metaphor for the immanent transcendence of poetic recollection, its magic combination of mirror and dream.

In the essays and poems the use of the starlight metaphor is even more striking. In speaking of the eternal quality of art, for instance, Hofmannsthal describes paintings out of which and "into us constantly flows the distant past in the form of the present, as if into a spacious basin. In these colors the reflection of a long-lost past strikes us, like the rays of a star long since reduced to dust" (PII, 24). In the poem "Manche freilich" (1895), a very similar image is used, and subtly associated with the image of the eye of the poet:

> Ganz vergessener Völker Müdigkeiten
> Kann ich nicht abtun von meinen Lidern
> Noch weghalten von der erschrockenen Seele
> Stummes Niederfallen ferner Sterne.   (G, 19)

Twelve years later, in his seminal address on "Der Dichter und diese Zeit," Hofmannsthal uses the very same metaphors of eye and star once more, again in an attempt to describe the magical process of poetic recollection: for the poet "the present is indescribably interwoven with the past: in the pores of his body he still feels the lived quality of past days, of distant ancestors never known . . . ; his eyes . . . still light upon . . . the living fire of stars that long ago were consumed by icy space" (PII, 245). The poet, for Hofmannsthal, is basically one who can never forget.

It might be well to point out here that Hofmannsthal's predilection for a symbolism of light, shadows, and reflection—and, as we shall soon see, for the cave as well—furnishes yet another aspect of his close relationship to Neoplatonism. From the time of Plato's Allegory of the Cave, metaphors of reflected, ethereal light and subterranean darkness have shaped the Neoplatonic tradition.[13] As indicated in the epigraph to this chapter, Plato would lead mortals from their unenlightened Cave toward the shining Ideas by first having them contemplate the "images of men and things reflected in water," and through these reflections they would pass to the reflections of the stars, and from these, to the very sun and stars themselves. Saint Paul, in much the same tradition, employs a similar metaphor when he speaks to the Corinthians of that glorious time when we shall no longer see God "through a glass, darkly," but rather face to face. And Plotinus, also preaching the reality of things unseen, constantly uses metaphors of heavenly brightness and luminosity and invokes the Center of Being as a radiant source that would shed light on all things. The tradition continues down through the "creating mirror" of Goethe,[14] Shelley's vision of poets as "mirrors of the gigantic

[13] For a summary of Neoplatonic aesthetics and the role of luminous metaphors within the tradition, see W. Wimsatt and C. Brooks, *Literary Criticism: A Short History* (New York, 1965), pp. 112-139; M. H. Abrams, *The Mirror and the Lamp: Romantic Theory and the Critical Tradition* (New York, 1958), pp. 42-46; and Monroe Beardsley, *Aesthetics from Classical Greece to the Present* (New York, 1966), pp. 78-88. It should also be noted at this point that Mircea Eliade, in his chapter "Experiences of the Mystic Light" in *The Two and the One* (London, 1965), indicates that the tradition of such images extends to Eastern religions as well, and thus hints that such metaphors may ultimately be archetypal.

[14] Cf. the paralipomena to *Faust*, where Faust asks Mephisto "wo der schaffende Spiegel sei" (*Gedenkausgabe der Werke, Briefe und Gespräche* [Zürich, 1962], v, 544); also Hofmannsthal's own note on

25

shadows which futurity casts upon the present,"[15] Wordsworth's invocation of "Those shadowy recollections,/ Which, be they what they may,/ Are yet the fountain-light of all our day,"[16] Baudelaire's "Correspondances" that answer one another like "prolonged echoes that merge far away/ In a deep and shadowy unity,/ As vast as darkness, as vast as light,"[17] and Rilke's vision in the Second Elegy of his angels as narcissistic mirrors.

In spite of his use of the traditional images and metaphors of Neoplatonism, Hofmannsthal, as we have already stressed, was not a Neoplatonist. In fact, we can read the story of his progressive disenchantment with the dream-like realm of poetic memory in the very images we have been referring to. For toward the end of his lyric decade Hofmannsthal's images of mirror and well chronicle, in almost unconscious fashion, his growing awareness of the dangers inherent in a life devoted solely to the magical moments of a passive, aesthetic communion with the past. Already in the early poem "Besitz" (1893), for instance, the poet, after a sudden vision of his garden "dreamily united" in its reflection in the garden pool, questions if such deep reflections can ever share their mystery with life. The thematic pattern of the dream-vision or reflection that leads not only

---

the fact that the human mind itself is a form of "schaffender Spiegel" (A, 183). Franz Koch, in his study of *Goethe und Plotin* (Leipzig, 1925), devotes an entire chapter to "der schaffende Spiegel."

[15] "A Defense of Poetry."

[16] "Intimations of Immortality from Recollections of Early Childhood."

[17] The French Symbolists were well known to Hofmannsthal through Stefan George, and there are fascinating parallels between their imagery and that of Hofmannsthal. See Georges Poulet's chapter on Mallarmé, for instance, in *The Interior Distance* (Baltimore, 1959), on the mirror and other images.

away from life but even into death is, in fact, extremely common in the early Hofmannsthal; the poem "Leben, Traum und Tod," the *Reitergeschichte*, and *Das kleine Welttheater*, are three prominent examples. In the last, the Madman (associated, in true Platonic fashion, with the poet), perched on a bridge at dusk and contemplating himself in a small silver handmirror, threatens to leap to his death in the stream below, which leads:

> . . . bis wo die letzten Meere
> Wie stille leere Spiegel stehen.   (G, 299)

"Der goldene Apfel," an undated prose fragment (1894?), demonstrates even more clearly the growing separation of the realm of timeless recollections from the world of the present. First of all, the image of the well in the story, which again symbolizes the entrance to a netherworld of memories and fairytale-like dreams, has suddenly been enlarged in an ominous fashion, for it now leads to a vast subterranean chamber that has a second entrance located in the street before the house. Furthermore, the well has dried up, and both entrances are sealed off by large stones—a fact reminiscent of the strange "recollected" girl in "Das Glück am Weg," who disappears in the end "as if one had put her into a small, narrow shaft, and over this a heavy stone" (Pl, 127).

The golden apple, accidentally discovered in the house by the small daughter, belongs in some mysterious way to this same underground realm, for in it is mixed an "excessive sweetness and tormenting desire" (E, 41). Yet the girl's attempts to gain access to the subterranean passageway fail, and the apple eventually falls into the hands of one of the king's royal grooms. Here the story breaks off, with notes hinting at a violent ending. The mysterious realms of magic

27

recollection—here associated with an Arabian Nights atmosphere of evil and exoticism (for the piece is clearly modelled on the tales of the nineteenth and twentieth *Arabian Nights*)—have become ominous as well as inaccessible.

This growing discrepancy between the oneiric realm of the poet and the brute reality of present experience is portrayed from the opposite point of view a few years later in the poem "Reiselied." In the first strophe of the poem, the poet evokes the tragic, devastating time of the present:

> Wasser stürzt, uns zu verschlingen,
> Rollt der Fels, uns zu erschlagen. . . .   (G, 11)

Time here, similar to the march of time in the *Reitergeschichte* and the gliding, senseless time of the "Ballade des äusseren Lebens," represents a meaningless movement towards death. In the second strophe, however, the poet directs his gaze inward and downward to a static realm of endless mirrors:

> Aber unten liegt ein Land,
> Früchte spiegelnd ohne Ende
> In den alterslosen Seen.

The ageless lakes, like the timeless seas yearned for by the Madman, represent the ultimate source of poetic remembrance, the long-forgotten "Weltgeheimnis," and, for a time at least, their magic power is vouchsafed to the poet once more. Much like the occasional person who can still invoke the word "evening" in the "Ballade," the poet stands in a protected garden—together with his marble statues, bright flowers, and magic well—and is uplifted for a time by dream-like remembrance:

> Marmorstirn und Brunnenrand
> Steigt aus blumigem Gelände,
> Und die leichten Winde wehn.

As implied elsewhere in Hofmannsthal, the images of well and marble were among those he associated with classical poetry (PII, 92); the "Reiselied," in its basic intent, is the song of an inner, poetic journey.

In "Reiselied" the dream-world is secured at the expense of a partial loss of reality in the poet. In *Das Bergwerk zu Falun*, begun the following year (1899), the subterranean realm of memory has noticeably widened from the original well to an immense cavern in the bowels of the earth, one even larger than that portrayed in "Der goldene Apfel." Furthermore, it can only be gained at the cost of the poet's own soul.[18] The individual memories that once were captured in the occasional reflection of an eye, in the mirroring of a pool, or in the dark surface of a well are now the province of the Mountain Queen, who emits the strange bright light of pure recollection. Her natural domain is the crystalline stream of all time; like the magician in the poet's "Traum von grosser Magie" she summons with a mere gesture all time past:

[18] Hofmannsthal's imagery of the well and the cave would doubtless prove fertile terrain for a Freudian, or even Jungian interpretation as well, Elis's journey to the Mountain Queen variously signifying, for instance, a retreat to the womb, to pre-existence, to the realm of dreams, or to the unconscious (in this case more to a Jungian *collective* unconscious than to a Freudian one). We should bear in mind, however, that the well and the cave also connect with another tradition—that of the romantics, extending from Novalis (fifth chapter of *Heinrich von Ofterdingen*), E.T.A. Hoffmann (*Falun*), and Coleridge (the "caverns measureless to man" in "Kubla Khan") through the French Symbolists down to George (*Algabal*). See Werner Vordtriede, *Novalis und die französischen Symbolisten* (Stuttgart, 1963), in particular the chapter "Das Unterreich." A further literary tradition that should be noted here is again the Neoplatonic, where caves and wells have also played an important role, from Plato's Allegory of the Cave and Porphyry's gloss on Homer's Cave of the Nymphs to the present day. See, for instance, Yeats's essay on "The Philosophy of Shelley's Poetry."

> das uralt heilige Gestern,
> Ruf ich es auf, umgibts mich und wird Heut:
> Und Dunkelndes und Funkelndes vergeht,
> Und längstversunknes blüht und glüht herein.
>
> (G, 356)

In short, she rules the Neoplatonic world of dream and memory, the absolute realm of the poet. Those who, like the hero Elis, come to serve the Queen, must assume one of two positions: either they become, like old Torbern, magicians or, in the manner of the servant Agmahd, merely reflecting mirrors (G, 363). There are no alternatives, for there is no way back from the mine.

Although *Das Bergwerk zu Falun* represents an absolute statement on the dangers of total commitment to the poetic vision, Hofmannsthal attempted to deal with the theme once more, in a fairy tale written at the turn of the century. The miner Hyacinth, the poet-hero of *Das Märchen von der verschleierten Frau*, is, unlike Elis, a married man with a young daughter. During his daily shift at the mine, Hyacinth is often overcome by intense memories of his own childhood—so much so that at times his very hammering itself appears to him to be "in the dream-like realm of memory" (E, 80). One day, when working in the mine, he is accosted by a young miner whom he has never seen before and who asks him: "Did you have to *recollect* strongly at your silent work today?" (E, 80; Hofmannsthal's italics). The young stranger thereupon leaves, with the parting remark that the Veiled Lady has been waiting for Hyacinth for some time now. On his way home from the mine that evening Hyacinth pauses for a moment on an old stone bridge over a dark stream to survey the landscape and to reflect upon the young stranger. In a scene that recalls that of "Reiselied" he pauses for a moment, suspended between the plunge of the stream and the high wall of rock rising above him; his gaze is drawn irresistibly downward. Yet the quiet landscape of ageless lakes portrayed in "Reiselied" has here been demonized: Hyacinth stares into a "damp, roaring abyss, as if . . . a secret door there would open up into the interior" (E, 79). He suddenly understands the deeper meaning of the "isolated, meaningless, and sweet memories from indistinct, earlier times of his life" (E, 80) that had so often assailed him in the mine, and he now knows that it is time. The eternal, inner spaces of memory and dream beckon to the poet who is caught in the midst of life and time.

That very night Hyacinth steals from the house, is greeted by the noise, not of "waterfalls and falling rocks" (E, 85) but of a huge coach driven by a satanic coachman, and is snatched away into the darkening valley to the realm of the Veiled Lady.[19] Here the story breaks off abruptly, and there follow a few brief notes concerning the projected ending of the tale. According to these Hyacinth does not, like Elis, remain forever with the Veiled Lady but eventually abjures the magic realm in order to assume once more his role as husband and father. Furthermore, he is to return through a well near his house—the very same well in which his wife had glimpsed a fearful vision on the morning of his departure into the abyss. The final images describing his return from the magic realm of memory, however, are even more striking than the image of the well, for as he first catches

---

[19] The poetic journey described here bears many parallels to that depicted in Hofmannsthal's poem "Ein Prolog" (1897), a symbolistic dream-allegory of the poetic process. There, for instance, the satanic side of the journey is also emphasized: in place of the coachman with his "rotfunkelndem Gesicht," the poet is accompanied by a "Knecht mit rotem Haar" (G, 128).

sight of his wife again in a *mirror*[20] she informs him that
their daughter had seen his return written in the *stars*.

Das Märchen von der verschleierten Frau thus brings to
a virtual close Hofmannsthal's long and uneasy alliance
with the egocentric dream-realm of poetic recollection. His
inability to finish the *Märchen* reveals not so much his
ambivalence toward the proposed ethical ending (the very
last word of the tale, in fact, is characteristically the word
"*Du*") as the immense difficulty involved in portraying a
renunciation of the subterranean lyric realm in a poetically
convincing manner—even when clothed in the imaginative
form of the fairy tale. The following year, 1901, Hofmannsthal himself, twenty-seven years old, was to marry, leave
his home in Vienna, and settle in a manor house at Rodaun,
withdrawing at the same time his application for a teaching
post in Romance languages at the University of Vienna. The
year after that he would write the well-known Chandos
Letter, the document that formally signalled the end of his
lyric decade. As we have attempted to show through the
images, however, this crisis of the aesthete, like all crises,
did not occur on a certain date and at a certain place, but
had been developing steadily throughout the previous ten
years. In the image of the magically reflecting well that de-

[20] In this image as well as in others Hofmannsthal's story bears a
striking resemblance to E.T.A. Hoffmann's *Märchen* "Die Abenteuer
der Silvesternacht," for in a chapter entitled "Die Geschichte vom
verlorenen Spiegelbild" Hoffmann also portrays a husband who deserts his wife and child for a demonic mistress-muse (Giulietta) in
a land of the poetic imagination (Italy). When he later leaves her,
however, he must pay with the loss of his *Spiegelbild*, his mirror-
reflection, and must henceforth wander through life bereft of his
shadow-self, an outcast both from art and from the everyday world
of his family. Apart from the ending, the story is essentially that of
Hofmannsthal's, and when we recall that Hofmannsthal during his
writing of the tale of Hyacinth was also occupied with a dramatiza-
tion of Hoffmann's story about Falun, the possibility of an influence
would seem quite strong.

velops into the satanic underground cavern is written the story of an increasingly ambivalent and problematic relationship to the lyrical, dream-like act of poetic recollection.

The growing dangers confronting the visionary poet who cannot reconcile the magical past with the concrete present (Elis), the dream with life (the Madman), or the reflection in the garden pool with the life outside the garden (the poet in "Besitz") are also evident in the image of the mirror itself. For already in his early letters Hofmannsthal gives evidence that he sensed the dangers inherent in the looking-glass of art and in its wellspring, memory: at one point, for instance, he complains that as a youth he had been alone too much with mirrors (BI, 71) and again, somewhat later, he notes the fact that the forces of life could infuse one's sense of beauty much in the same manner that tarnish can cover a mirror (BI, 243). Similarly, in an essay of 1897, he concludes that "whoever has much to do with mirror images will never be very inclined, in questions of good and evil, to believe in anything permanent" (PI, 287). The most striking instance of all, however, occurs in *Der Kaiser und die Hexe*, Hofmannsthal's lyrical drama of the same year, in which, in one of the most moving scenes, the Emperor warns his young chamberlain of the dangers of the magic mirror of youth:

> Nimm du dich in acht, das Leben
> Hat die rätselhafte Kraft,
> Irgendwie von einem Punkt aus
> Diesen ganzen Glanz der Jugend
> Zu zerstören, blinden Rost
> Auszustreuen auf diesen Spiegel
> Gottes. . . .   (G, 265)

Two   The Aesthetic Adventurer:

The Past as Assailant

> The more the personality disappears in the twilight of
> mood, so much the more is the individual in the moment,
> and this, again, is the most adequate expression for the
> aesthetic existence: it is in the moment.[21]

HE TALE of the poet with his magic mirror constitutes only one half of the story of memory in
Hofmannsthal; the other concerns the poet's constant
counterpart in the early poems and plays—the figure of
the aesthetic adventurer. For at the side of Hofmannsthal's young rememberer there inevitably ranges the
figure of the youth who is totally involved with the landscape of the present moment:

> Ihm fiel nicht ein, den Reichtum seiner Seele,
> Die frühern Wege und Erinnerung
> Verschlungner Finger und getauschter Seelen
> Für mehr als nichtigen Besitz zu achten.

(G, 27)

Whereas the poet serves art—the dream of the past—the
adventurer is beholden to life and its golden dream of
the present. Bright impressions of the moment veil remembered images of the past, and a sense of transport,
of floating upon time, replaces the sensation of disappearing, like Elis and Hyacinth, beneath time's surface.
The adventurer, in his best moments, is suspended above
the abyss of being merely by the euphoria of the present

[21] Sören Kierkegaard, *Either/Or* (Garden City, N.Y., 1959), II,
234.

moment; he becomes an heir of the past who squanders munificently the riches of his inheritance:

> Den Erben lass verschwenden
> An Adler, Lamm und Pfau
> Das Salböl aus den Händen
> Der toten alten Frau!
>
> . . . .
>
> Er lächelt der Gefährten.—
> Die schwebend unbeschwerten
> Abgründe und die Gärten
> Des Lebens tragen ihn.   (G, 12-13)

The adventurer, with his Faustian dedication to the freshness of each new moment, belongs not only to the Viennese cult of the viveur, the dandy, and the decadent, but also to the world of late nineteenth-century impressionism.[22] Certain of Hofmannsthal's early poems, even when the figure of the adventurer is absent, are pure evocations of this mood of momentary impressions; a lyric on the images of early spring, for example, with its description of wind catching hair and blossoms:

> Er [the wind] hat sich gewiegt,
> Wo Weinen war,
> Und hat sich geschmiegt
> In zerrüttetes Haar.
>
> Er schüttelte nieder
> Akazienblüten
> . . . .   (G, 7)

is pure Pissarro turned to poetry, just as is "Juniabend im Volksgarten" (PI, 187), with its evocation of white chest-

---

[22] See Richard Alewyn, *Über Hugo von Hofmannsthal* (Göttingen, 1963), pp. 51-56, 99, 109, 112-119, 156, 186.

nuts in bloom in a city park. In answer to the poet's assertion that "it is memory that makes us gods," as Cesarino
states in *Der Abenteurer und die Sängerin* (1898), echoing
Neoplatonic thought, the impressionistic adventurer merely
replies, like the older Baron, that "the moment is everything" (DI, 451). Life for the adventurer means to bask in
the light of immediate consciousness; dedicated to the
mysteries of the visible world, he luxuriates in the realm of
appearance.[23]

Yet there also exists a dark side to the adventurer, and in
this one respect he approaches his counterpart the poet. For
the poet, lacking any real dimension in the present, also
lacks a true self; he is a chameleon who is constant prey to
the shades of reminiscence. The adventurer, on the other
hand, having no hold on the past and thus possessing no history, also has no real self. Like the figures in an impression-
ist painting, he tends to dissolve, upon closer analysis, into
a multitude of isolated points and momentary impressions.
On becoming conscious of this fact, he is overcome by a
baroque horror at the nothingness of the supposed self and
by a modern despair over the illusory nature of what we
normally call the personality. The latter mood is a particularly common one in Hofmannsthal's early poems and plays,
as in the "Terzinen über Vergänglichkeit," where the poet
invokes the bewildering frailty of the self:

> Dies ist ein Ding, das keiner voll aussinnt,
> Und viel zu grauenvoll, als dass man klage:
> Dass alles gleitet und vorüberrinnt.

[23] The question of impressionism in literature as well as the arts is,
of course, a vast topic, to which many single studies have been devoted, one of the best being R. Hamann and J. Hermand, *Impressionismus* (Berlin, 1966).

Und dass mein eignes Ich, durch nichts gehemmt,
Herüberglitt aus einem kleinen Kind
Mir wie ein Hund unheimlich stumm und fremd.

(G, 17)[24]

This saddening discovery by the poet, as well as by the adventurer, that the self is but a transitory illusion might best be described by comparing it to what Kierkegaard termed the despair that must ultimately result from the aesthetic mode of existence. For "in mood," as Kierkegaard says (and the aesthete, like Don Juan, lives only for the sensuous mood of the moment), "the personality is . . . but . . . dimly present."[25] It is the same insight that Hofmannsthal himself reached very early, as is evidenced by his essay on Walter Pater (1894), in particular by his comments on Pater's *Marius the Epicurean.*

In considering the relationship between Hofmannsthal's figure of the adventurer and the worlds of Kierkegaard, the French impressionists, Pater, and the English Pre-Raphaelites, we have omitted one of the most striking influences on the Viennese intellectual climate of the time. The figure is Ernst Mach, the Viennese psychologist, physicist, and metaphysician whose philosophy Hermann Bahr termed ex-

[24] The end of the poem, in a dialectical reversal akin to that found at the end of some of the early plays, actually asserts the reality of an ancestral self, and will be discussed below (p. 76) in connection with the importance of memory; the poem is a perfect example of the way in which opposing themes so often run parallel to one another in Hofmannsthal.

[25] Kierkegaard, *Either/Or*, II, 234. As pointed out below (pp. 90 ff.), the extraordinary parallels between Kierkegaard and Hofmannsthal, in particular with regard to their thoughts on time and memory, obviously prepared the way for Hofmannsthal's later, and documented, use of Kierkegaard as a source for some of his writings. Both writers, for example, viewed the ultimate despair of the aesthete as necessarily leading to a higher, ethical stage of existence.

pressly the "philosophy of impressionism."[26] Although he
is probably best-known today for the supersonic Mach
numbers in physics, Mach was an extraordinarily versatile
thinker, whose writings have influenced such various men
as Einstein, Freud, William James, and Robert Musil. Although Hofmannsthal did not attend Mach's lectures at the
University of Vienna until 1897, it is very possible that he
had come into contact with some of his ideas before then,
for Mach's seminal work, *Die Analyse der Empfindungen*,
had been published in 1886 and was so popular that it had
gone into four editions by 1902. Basically, Mach's impressionistic philosophy postulated a world that was neither
mental nor material, subjective nor objective, but rather
composed of neutral elements called sensations (*Empfindungen*). In Mach's view all previous dualisms and dialec-
tics of German metaphysics, from the Platonic antithesis of
reality and appearance to the "monstrous" Kantian
dichotomy of self and things-in-themselves, dissolve (as
they do in the empiricist philosophy of Hume, an avowed
forerunner of Mach's) into a monistic system of glittering
sensations. Much as in the world of Pissarro, Monet, and
Seurat, the subject-object plane dissolves into a sea of
many-colored points, so much so that the personality itself
becomes nothing more than a sum of atomistic, "objective"
sensations without an organizing center. The ego, for Mach,
is "as little absolutely permanent as our bodies. That which
we so much dread in death, the annihilation of our perma-
nency, actually occurs in life in abundant measure. . . . The
assumption, or postulation, of the ego," he concludes, quoting Lichtenberg, "is a mere practical necessity."[27]

[26] Hermann Bahr, "Philosophie des Impressionismus," in *Dialog
vom Tragischen* (Berlin, 1904), p. 114.

[27] Ernst Mach, *The Analysis of Sensations*, trans. C. M. Williams
(New York, 1959), pp. 6, 4, 29.

The parallel between Mach's thought and Hofmannsthal's poetry should be clear: the emphasis on life as a series of impressions or sensations, the illusory quality of the self, and the resultant dependency upon sheer memory for the proof of personality are common to both writers.[28] Mach's remarks on memory at one point could be straight from the poet of the third strophe of the "Terzinen": "When I recall today my early youth, I should take the boy that I then was, with the exception of a few individual features, for a different person, were it not for the existence of the chain of memories."[29] In fact, the young protagonist of Hofmannsthal's first lyric drama *Gestern*, written when he was only seventeen, actually furnishes a striking example of the impressionistic, Machian type of adventurer.[30] In the very first scene, while conversing with his lover Arlette, Andrea proclaims his cult of sensations, his credo of the aesthetic mood and the moment:

> Das Gestern lügt und nur das Heut ist wahr!
> Lass dich von jedem Augenblicke treiben,
> Das ist der Weg, dir selber treu zu bleiben;
> Der Stimmung folg, die deiner niemals harrt,
> Gib dich ihr hin, wo wirst du dich bewahren.
>
> (G, 149)

The lines, however, like Mephisto's sharp comment to Faust,

> Da ist's vorbei. Was ist daran zu lesen?
> Es ist so gut als wäre es nie gewesen,[31]

[28] Gotthart Wunberg has a good discussion of the parallels between Hofmannsthal and Mach in his *Der frühe Hofmannsthal: Schizophrenie als dichterische Struktur* (Stuttgart: Kohlhammer, 1965), pp. 23-44.

[29] Mach, p. 4.

[30] I would like to call attention here to Alewyn's excellent treatment of the play in *Über Hugo von Hofmannsthal*, pp. 46-63.

[31] Lines 11, 600 ff.

betray the ethical nihilism that lies at the heart of the impressionistic style of life when it becomes absolute. In a life dominated by what Kierkegaard called aesthetic mood the "two souls" of the Faustian adventurer have been split asunder into an infinity of Machian sensations:

> Erwacht und stirbt nicht jede Leidenschaft?
> Wer lehrte uns, den Namen "Seele" geben
> Dem Beieinandersein von tausend Leben?
>
> (G, 155)

For Andrea the self has become, as Hofmannsthal puts it in one of his essays, a mere "metaphor, an illusory rainbow, a dovecote of moods and sensations that continually come and go" (PII, 83). The real existence of the personality, in Andrea's eyes, lies as much outside ourselves as within:

> Ist nicht die ganze ewige Natur
> Nur ein Symbol für unsrer Seelen Launen?
> Was suchen wir in ihr als unsre Spur?
> Und wird uns alles nicht zum Gleichnisbronnen
> Uns auszudrücken, unsre Qual und Wonnen?
>
> (G, 167)

As the play progresses, however, Andrea gradually awakens to the force of past time, of "yesterday." What he had earlier preached (in the paratactic style characteristic of the adventurer's own disconnected life style),

> Und vorwärts reicht kein Wissen, noch zurück!
> Und jeder ist des Augenblickes Knecht,
> Und nur das Jetzt, das Heut, das Hier hat Recht!
>
> (G, 174)

is suddenly put into practice by Arlette herself, for she deserts Andrea for another. In the tenth and final scene, she shocks him with the news, in words that recall those of the "Terzinen über Vergänglichkeit":

Ein Abgrund scheint von gestern mich zu trennen,
Und fremd steh ich mir selber gegenüber . . .

. . . .

Vergib, vergiss dies Gestern, lass mich bleiben,
Lass Nächte drübergleiten, Tage treiben. . . .

(G, 179)

For the first time in his life Andrea, in becoming conscious
of another self, also becomes conscious of the ineluctable
continuity of his own, and his sense of time suddenly
reaches out beyond the shallow buoyancy of the present:

Dies Gestern ist so eins mit deinem Sein,
Du kannst es nicht verwischen, nicht vergessen:
Es ist, so lang wir wissen, dass es war.

. . . .

Was einmal war, das lebt auch ewig fort.

(G, 179)

And thus the playlet closes. As its ironic title implies, the
hero of the piece is not Andrea, but past time itself, for the
sense of duration asserts itself at the end with intense, compelling force.

Gestern is, in many ways, paradigmatic with regard to
the theme of the impressionistic mode of existence as portrayed in Hofmannsthal's early works. For in most of these
the hero's Faust-like attempt to thwart time and to live in
the continuous moment of the present is ultimately repaid
by the sudden intrusion of vengeful memories. The past, in
a very real sense, becomes an assailant. Although it is true
that in a few of the poems—such as "Lebenslied" and "Der
Jüngling in der Landschaft"—a euphoric unity in the present is successfully maintained, the egregious attempt to refute time and memory usually fails, and is repaid again and
again by an avenging past, either in the form of another

41

person or in the form of memories, as hypermnesia. In fact, the phenomenon of hypermnesia—of having one's entire life or part of one's life pass in front of one's eyes, particularly in a moment of danger—is one that Hofmannsthal himself mentions in his journal. Following a note in the style of the adventurer, "My self of yesterday concerns me as little as does that of Napoleon or Goethe," and apparently written half a year later, comes the inevitable antithesis, a jotting on "the awakening of memory (hypermnesia) in dreams, in sickness, in danger, in the hour of death" (A, 93).[32]

Hypermnesia in the hour of death actually occurs in several of Hofmannsthal's early writings. The most dramatic examples are undoubtedly in the verse play *Der Tor und der Tod* (1893) and the novella *Reitergeschichte* (1898), in both of which the pattern of suppression and then release of past time emerges with singular clarity. Claudio, the aesthetic young aristocrat in the former, is the counterpart of Andrea in *Gestern*: a creature of mood who lives only for himself and the sensation of the moment. Yet Claudio, true to his name (*claudere*), is actually an introverted Andrea, for he leads a life of sequestered self-centeredness. Until the evening of his death (when the play opens) he has been aware of only the present, his disregard of the past obviously being motivated by a fear of facing the reality of the future and of death. He has lived his life, as he admits, like a half-read book—half as yet unseen, half no longer understood (G, 204). At Death's unexpected entrance, however, his past wells up within him in poignant visions of his lonely mother, his neglected lover, and a friend whom he had betrayed. Much as in *Gestern*, the close of the play brings the

---

[32] Hermann Broch's long novel, *Der Tod des Vergil*, centers, interestingly enough, on this same phenomenon: Virgil, faced with death, recollects and reflects on his past life.

dialectical reversal of the ethic that has been preached up to this point: the sudden recognition of the past's constant obtrusion upon the present brings with it the deeper ethical insight that the lives of others are inseparable from our own. Claudio's key confession,

> Ich will die Treue lernen, die der Halt
> Von allem Leben ist . . .   (G, 211)

is a pledge to honor the I *and* the Thou.

The fate of Anton Lerch, the cavalry sergeant in *Reitergeschichte*, is another variation on the same tragic theme; he is, in effect, a Claudio who has been wrenched from the easy life of selfish comforts to be confronted with the intolerable realities of war, time, and death. In the course of a single day's sporadic fighting during the Italian wars of 1848, Lerch, through a strange encounter with a village woman, becomes increasingly enmeshed in a web of past memories and future hopes that completely divorce him from all present reality. Aroused by the fortuitous encounter with Vuic, the woman in the village, he loses himself in memories of sensuous Viennese nights and dreams of the warm complacencies of a snug bourgeois existence. Several hours after passing through the village Lerch suddenly experiences the dreams once more, this time with renewed force. He is filled with both a "thirst for unexpected gain, for gratification" (E, 54) and a yearning for Vuic's comfortable room, with its "mahogany furniture and the pots of basil" (E, 53), and the sudden capture of an enemy horse merely draws him further into worlds beyond the present.

With unerring dramatic logic, however, the scenes of Lerch's visions contrast tragically with the destructive march of military time, an antithesis perfectly rendered by the image of a "slippered life with the hilt of his sabre sticking through the left pocket of his dressing-gown" (E, 54), and at the end of the same day he is executed for refusing to hand over the horse he had taken. Whether it is the foreknowledge of death that brings these final visions and dreams (hypermnesia in the face of death) or whether it is merely that the visions themselves, in a realistic manner, hinder his ability to obey, is impossible to say. The fact that the unity of the piece lies more in its dream-like images than in its themes or "plot" would, however, seem to exclude the latter.[33] In either case, the important fact from our point of view is that Lerch, like Claudio, fails to integrate the present moment with past and future. Only through a constant awareness of the past, accompanied by a constant re-ordering and sublimation of recollected experience, can we achieve, in Hofmannsthal's eyes, a proper relationship to the present and the future. When Lerch is shot and falls to the ground he appropriately falls *between* the two horses—between the highly prized dream-horse, "young, vain, beautiful" (E, 60), and the everyday horse of his regiment. In this last mute gesture, the split in his existence becomes tragically evident.

The sudden revival of vivid memories from the distant past (the actual experience with Vuic in Vienna had occurred some ten years before the Italian encounter) is not confined to the figures of Claudio and Lerch alone; it also appears in many of Hofmannsthal's poems. Very often the memories of the past self actually assume the form of a *Doppelgänger* or alter ego, a ghost from the past who revisits the self after many years of neglect. (Lerch's *Doppelgänger*, as in traditional folk superstitions, is a doubling of his *present* self and thus a sign of impending death.) In the

---

[33] William R. Donop, in his "Archetypal Vision in Hofmannsthal's *Reitergeschichte*," *German Life and Letters*, 22 (1969), 126-134, gives an excellent Jungian interpretation of the images in the story.

"Terzinen," for instance—which we have already quoted—
the poet, caught in the impressionistic flux of time, suddenly
catches a glimpse of himself as a child, years before, and the
contrast with his present self produces a poignant sense of
distance akin to that which we sense when in the presence
of an animal. The two worlds, though proximate, are separated by an infinity. Similarly, in "Erlebnis" the young
poet, much like Claudio, upon hearing the music of death
experiences an unexpected and inexplicable yearning for
his past—expressed in the poem through the simile of one
on a boat who suddenly perceives himself as a child standing on the shore. And again, in "Vor Tag" the youth suddenly becomes aware of having passed from childhood into
the harsh daylight of maturity, self-consciousness, and sin
(following his first night with a woman) when he catches
sight of himself in a mirror and discovers that a stranger has
"murdered" the boy that he once was. And just as this youth
feels himself to be a "thief" stealing in through his own window, so the Madman-poet in *Das kleine Welttheater*, even
more prey to schizophrenic dislocations of the self in time,
senses at one point

> . . . auf der eigenen Stirn die Spur
> Der eignen Sohle, von mir selber fort
> Mich schwingend wie ein Dieb aus einem Fenster.
>
> (G, 315)

Like the images of eye and mirror, the window image—
often of the bedroom, the transitional realm of dreams—is
frequently used by Hofmannsthal to express his juxtaposition of two existences, as in "Erlebnis" (G, 9) and *Das
Märchen von der verschleierten Frau* (E, 85). The axiom
of much of Hofmannsthal's early prose and poetry is none
other than the insight that Mach had had some time earlier,

45

that "there can hardly be greater differences in the egos of different people than occur in the course of years in one person."[34]

The encounter with the *Doppelgänger*, the involuntary memory of a past self, conceals within it a sinister aspect, however. As much as Hofmannsthal was fascinated by such creatures of the moment as children, adventurers, actors, and dancers, with their chameleon-like gift for constant change[35] (an ability he himself, like Goethe, obviously possessed to a considerable degree), he also realized, far more than most poets, the ultimate dangers inherent in such a way of life. Whereas a poet such as Yeats, for example, viewed masks as dialectically necessary for a cognitive grasp of the personality, Hofmannsthal saw in them, on the one hand, an expression of pure childlike delight in disguise and metamorphosis and yet, on the other, their possible pathological aspect—the danger of losing one's true personality entirely among the various different poses. At the close of *Der weisse Fächer* (1897), for instance, Miranda's bold words celebrating her return to life actually betray the hubris of the adventurer, the Machian conviction that the "ego is as little absolutely permanent as are bodies":[36]

> Ich selbst mit meinem eignen Selbst von früher,
> Von einer Stunde früher grad so nah,
> Vielmehr so fern verwandt, als mit dem Vogel,
> Der dort hinflattert. (G, 252)

Amid life's many-colored, transitory, and pointillistic aspects the sense of the self is completely lost:

> . . . wir selber nur der Raum,
> Drin Tausende von Träumen buntes Spiel

---

[34] Mach, p. 3. [35] See Chapter 10. [36] Mach, p. 4.

So treiben wie im Springbrunn Myriaden
Von immer neuen, immer fremden Tropfen.

(G, 252)

The last and most significant of the aesthetic adventurers
in Hofmannsthal's early works is the figure of Lord Chandos, the fictional twenty-six-year-old Elizabethan nobleman
and poet who writes to Francis Bacon in an attempt to explain the crisis that has led to his literary silence of the past
two years. Chandos, who in his youth had experienced life,
physically and spiritually, in a "state of continual intoxica-
tion . . . as one great unity" (PII, 10), has suddenly been
struck by the realization that words—particularly abstract
words, and thus thought—carry no existential weight what-
soever. Yet the crisis is not, as several critics have attempted
to demonstrate, one of language alone; it also represents in
large measure one of Hofmannsthal's strongest statements
on the crisis of the impressionistic self. Chandos represents
a more interesting case than the figures we have previously
discussed because of his extreme complexity. Although he
is a poet (a rememberer) and also married, he approaches
his opposite, the adventurer, in that he too lacks a fixed personality. Hofmannsthal, like Kierkegaard and Keats, viewed
the aesthetic existence as essentially a chameleon one, possessing no fixed value. Hofmannsthal, in fact, was acquainted with Keats's famous letter of October 27, 1818, in
which Keats stressed the tragic and inevitable lack of identity in the endlessly role-playing poet.[37] Indeed, one of
Chandos' most cherished dreams as a writer had been to
transform himself and to "disappear" into such mythical
personages of the past as Proteus, Perseus, and Acteon, to
"speak out of them with tongues" (PII, 9), as he puts it—a

[37] See BII, 254.

theme of metamorphosis that is also mirrored in the very form of the letter itself, for Hofmannsthal's prose abounds in impressionistic metaphors of color and movement.

In his letter Chandos confesses that approximately two years earlier everything for him had "disintegrated into fragments, those fragments again into fragments; no longer would anything let itself be encompassed by one idea" (PII, 13). Behind these words lies not only the existential despair Kierkegaard had prophesied for the aesthetic existence once it had become conscious of itself, but also a pathologically Machian revolt against such specious abstractions as ego and body: Chandos suffers from an "inexplicable uneasiness at even uttering the words 'spirit,' 'soul,' or 'body'" (PII, 11-12). What Mach preaches—"the self must be given up"—Chandos is forced to live, and life thus becomes for him a succession of isolated moments, the self an array of pointillistic fragments.[38]

In effect, then, Chandos is one of the earlier Faustian apostles of change who has now grown older, an Andrea or Claudio who has been condemned to live the life he had earlier preached. Although Chandos would attribute his crisis to a failure of words and concepts almost as if, in a romantic sense, language possessed an organic existence independent of the writer, his diagnosis of the crisis of words is at bottom a diagnosis of his own self. As the eloquent prose of his letter so ironically testifies, it is not the

---

[38] The problems touched upon in this paragraph are obviously more complex than indicated: Wunberg, who also points to the connections between Chandos and Mach in *Der frühe Hofmannsthal* (pp. 113-114, 117), views Chandos' crisis as primarily an epistemological one, i.e., as a crisis of "Objektverlust" (p. 113). The question of which came first, however—the loss of object, of self, or of the word—is at best wrongly stated and at worst infinitely debatable; the obvious answer would have to be that the terms are dialectically related to one another.

structure of syntax that is threatening to fracture and dis-
integrate, but the precarious identity of the self. This point
is dramatically made, not so much by the particular words
that cause him the most discomfort—"spirit, soul, body"—
as by the very title of the major work he had abandoned at
the onset of his crisis: *Nosce te ipsum* (PII, 10).

THREE   The Recollected Self: Three Epiphanies

T HE IMPRESSIONISTIC fragmentation of life and the word that Lord Chandos experiences represents a final position neither for Hofmannsthal nor indeed for Lord Chandos himself. For even the black despair that has surrounded him during the two years of his crisis has been pierced by occasional moments of light, moments in which the wholeness of things reasserts itself in compelling fashion. He describes these moments in the letter to Francis Bacon, and his words (which do not, as he would imply, desert him at this point) depict experiences that are essentially mystical illuminations. One evening, he writes, when he discovered in the shadow of a nut tree "a half-filled watering can . . . and a beetle in it, swimming on the surface from one dark shore to the other," he found that "this combination of trifles" sent through him "such a shudder at the presence of the infinite" that he wanted to break into words. Even now, "after weeks," he continues, "catching sight of that nut tree, I pass by it with a shy sidelong glance, for I am loath to dispel the memory of the miracle hovering there around the trunk." Concluding, he explains that in such moments as these, "an insignificant creature—a dog, a rat, a beetle, a crippled apple tree, a lane winding over the hill, a moss-covered stone, mean more to me than the most beautiful, most devoted mistress of the happiest night" (PII, 16).

Unlike most moments of mystical revelation, however, in which the soul's position in the universe is sanctified, Chandos' experience is characterized by a complete annihilation of the self; his feeling is one of total empathy, of "emptying" himself into the object. "It was," he writes, "far more and far less than sympathy: an immense participation, a flowing over into these creatures" (PII, 15), as though his body consisted of "nothing but ciphers that give me the key to everything" (PII, 17). The moments are also strangely devoid of any form of absolute transcendence, for they exclude both past and future and are dominated completely by the present moment and the object at hand: "It was the present," Chandos writes, "the fullest, most exalted present" (PII, 15). The experience for him is, paradoxically, one of an *immanent* transcendence, a "presence of the infinite" (PII, 16).[39] These ineffable moments of insight are for Chandos a form of secular revelation, for during them it is as if certain objects were inhabited by a sudden grace, and it is these moments of deep, ecstatic communion that remain his only hold on a fleeting, fragmentary, and chaotic world. "Apart from these strange occurrences," he adds, "which, incidentally, I hardly know whether to ascribe to the mind or the body, I live a life of barely believable emptiness, and have difficulties in concealing from my wife this inner stagnation" (PII, 17).

Viewed from the standpoint of literary history, Chandos' mystical moments connect with a more general phenomenon that was prevalent at the turn of the century. Hermann Bahr, Hofmannsthal's Viennese contemporary, describes

[39] In his essay "Wert und Ehre deutscher Sprache," Hofmannsthal quotes a passage from Kierkegaard that would indicate a similar concept of the visionary moment, the idea that "the eternal also designates that which is present and has no future, and this is the perfection of the eternal" (PIV, 438).

the very same experience in his essay "Ecstasy" in 1904.
"Ecstasy," Bahr writes, "is not merely a higher stage of good
humor, as people often seem to think nowadays. . . . There
belongs to ecstasy a feeling that a happy frame of mind
does not know, the blissfully painful feeling no longer to be
the same person, to leave oneself, to step outside oneself
(therefore 'ek-stasis')."[40] (We might add that Ernst Mach
had in part prophesied the same when he observed that the
self, "in our very happiest moments, may be partially or
wholly absent.")[41] This momentary feeling is, moreover,
likened by Bahr to the magic transfiguration experienced
by early Greek actors during the epiphany of Dionysus:
"the 'falling-together with God,' as Plotinus calls it . . . the
union mystica that the saints desire."[42] In his study of the
modern novel, Theodore Ziolkowski has commented on the
same phenomenon, pointing out that such epiphanies or private spiritual experiences are far from being limited to Austrian literature. "The great moments of modern literature"
in general "are instants of a sudden, intense, almost blind-
ingly vivid perception: what Virginia Woolf in *The Waves*
called 'rings of light.' Wherever we look," he continues, "we
are confronted with these moments of revelation. Joyce
called them epiphanies, and his works are in one sense a
catalogue of these moments of Thomist *claritas*."[43]

Viewed from within the span of Hofmannsthal's work itself, however, the Lord Chandos letter, with its portrayal
of such wordless, redemptive epiphanies, cannot be fully
understood or appreciated without a consideration of two

[40] Cf. the Madman in *Das kleine Welttheater* (1897), who also
experiences just such privileged moments of ecstasy (G, 315).

[41] Mach, p. 25.

[42] Bahr, "Ekstase," in *Dialog vom Tragischen*, pp. 136-138.

[43] Theodore Ziolkowski, *Dimensions of the Modern Novel* (Princeton, 1969), p. 212. See also Abrams' excellent treatment of the "Varieties of the Modern Moment" in *Natural Supernaturalism*, pp. 418-427.

later essays—the "Briefe des Zurückgekehrten" (1907) and the "Augenblicke in Griechenland" (1908-1914). In both of these, the problem of the dissociation of personality and perception is also overcome by the experiencing of a spiritual epiphany, yet an epiphany that includes an increasing awareness of self. The former essay, written some five years after the Chandos letter, is a brilliant and unusual work consisting of five fictitious letters. They are addressed, like the Chandos letter, to an English friend, and yet they are "contemporary," being written by a forty-year-old Austrian businessman who has returned home—symbolically at the turn of the century—after eighteen years spent on business in other parts of the world. The theme of the letters, which he writes in the spring of 1901, parallels that of the Chandos letter so closely that we can almost speak of the "Homecomer" as being an older Chandos. Yet whereas Chandos' voice had been the voice of a private catastrophe of the writer, the Homecomer speaks in terms of a European crisis, one that is invading Germany and Austria in particular. What is missing, in his eyes, is obviously difficult for him to describe; he continually reaches for the word *Ganzheit* (wholeness) to recapture that which has disappeared from the scene since the 1880's. The fragmentation of cultural traditions is perhaps what bothers him most: a live sense of the past has been replaced on the one hand by the pedantry of scholars, on the other by the events of yesterday's paper; the whole man, as he puts it, no longer moves at once.[44]

Yet the Homecomer, like Chandos, is also rescued from his existential unease by moments of grace, by glimpses of spiritual restoration. One day, for instance, while at an

[44] That "the whole man move together" (or that "the whole man must move at once") was one of Hofmannsthal's favorite adages, which he had borrowed, by way of Lichtenberg, from Addison and Steele (*The Spectator*, 6, 7 March 1711). Cf. (A, 151), PIII, 111), (PIV, 409).

exhibition of Van Gogh paintings, he experiences a sudden vision of that ideal ("grosser Hintergedanke") that is so tragically absent from contemporary European life: "that which was actually within the paintings, the essence, the indescribable sense of fate—all this I saw in such a way that I lost the sense of myself in the paintings, regained it powerfully, and lost it again!" (PII, 302-303). The epiphany, however, is decidedly different in quality from those of Lord Chandos, for in the Homecomer's experience there is notably no loss of self-consciousness; the "flowing" movement into the object has been transformed into a dialogue between object and self; the sensation, as he describes it (writing of another such experience previous to his return to Europe), is a "sacred enjoyment of my self and, at the same time, of the world." The increased self-consciousness is accompanied, moreover, by an expanded consciousness of time as well, for the experience synthesizes past and future into an "inexhaustible present" (PII, 308).

Furthermore, in remarking on what Chandos had termed the magic unity of childhood, the Homecomer points specifically to the role memory plays in this apparent unity of all early experience. He explains how, in his childhood, the world of memory and imagination—that of Dürer engravings, legends, fairy tales, and tales of ancestors—was totally indistinguishable from the realities of everyday life: "Everything in the old pictures was different from the reality before my eyes; but there was no break between the two. That older world was more pious, noble, gentle, bold, lonely. But there were paths in the forest, in the starry night, in the church, which led to that world" (PII, 295-296). Whereas Chandos had portrayed this childhood unity as a synthesis of the world within and that without—"a spiritual and a physical world" (PII, 10)—the Homecomer views it rather as a convergence of times, of past with present. It is, moreover, this magic sense of temporal unity in childhood that not only forms our adult sense of reality but also becomes our touchstone for that "reality behind the mundane" that he so tragically misses in Europe: "for there was something forcing me to measure reality against something within me, and almost unconsciously I measured it against that fearfully exalted, magical realm, testing everything on this touchstone to see if it was gold or merely a worthless yellow substitute" (PII, 296). The ultimate reality of the world emerges only through the constant interpretive act of testing each experience against the memories of childhood.

It is interesting to note that there are also several parallels between the letters of the Homecomer and *Andreas*, which was also begun in the same year (1907). Not only is Andreas twenty-two, the age at which the Homecomer left on his world *Bildungsreise*, and Sacramozo forty, precisely the age at which the Homecomer returns, but there are also reasons to believe that Hofmannsthal had originally intended to expand the letters into a short, epistolary Bildungsroman, one that was to have culminated in the marriage of the Homecomer;[45] in a sense, then, *Andreas* took the place of this Bildungsroman. Moreover, both works also share the important theme of memory, something that also relates them in turn to Hofmannsthal's essay on Greece.

The very title of the three-part essay "Augenblicke in Griechenland" suggests the momentary experience of an epiphany. Part lyrical landscape sketch, part travel diary, the essay represents the fruit of Hofmannsthal's visit in 1908 to Greece together with his friend Count Kessler and the French sculptor Maillol. It depicts in its final section, entitled "Die Statuen," a powerful mystical experience the

[45] See Mary Gilbert, "Hofmannsthal's Essays, 1900-1908. A Poet in Transition," in *Hofmannsthal, Studies in Commemoration*, ed. F. Norman (London, 1963), p. 33.

anonymous traveler-narrator has in Athens. Deciding one evening to climb alone to the top of the Acropolis, he has no sooner set out than he is assailed by an infinite sadness because Greece, despite the beauties of its ruins and its landscape, is doomed to remain forever a thing of the past, distant and foreign. His attempt to recollect the times and ways of the Greeks only entangles him in memories: "I attempted to remember," he explains, "but I could only remember memories, like mirrors reflecting more mirrors, endlessly" (PIII, 29). His despair resembles that of the Homecomer, to whom real trees on village squares were only memories of trees, and yet whereas the Homecomer had been concerned with overcoming a time-lapse of only twenty years, the traveler in Greece faces an abyss of two thousand. His despair, in fact, is nothing less than a despair over the fact of time itself: "It was nothing other than the curse of transcience . . . the small word 'past,'" he writes, "was stronger than the whole world" (PIII, 29).

The traveler's despair does not go unredeemed, however, for in a small museum near the Parthenon he comes upon the ancient statues of five Greek maidens,[46] and much like the Homecomer in front of the paintings of Van Gogh, he pauses for a moment to stare at them. Suddenly, while contemplating in the half-light of the small room the strange inner life he finds registered in their stony eyelids, he is seized by an intense vision of terror and bliss, arising within him like lightning from an abyss: a brightness far

[46] The statues Hofmannsthal saw, which were first discovered in 1885 and which are still in the museum today, are those of the maidens or *korai*, the young Greek priestesses he describes in his later essay on Greece (PIV, 160; 1922). Dating from the Archaic period (ca. 500 B.C.), they betray in their large eyes and enigmatic smiles a quality that is stylized and yet startlingly real. A photograph of one of them, given to Hofmannsthal by Helene von Nostitz, hung for a time in his study.

brighter than the light of day fills the room, and he suddenly experiences the glances of the statues as frighteningly
real. Unlike Chandos and the Homecomer, however, whose
epiphanies are in the present, he is virtually transported
back two thousand years into the past: "I am not seeing
these for the first time," he states. "In some way, in some
other world, I have stood in front of them before"
(PIII, 36).[47] The beauty and reality of the statues press
upon him with such force that he experiences them, in a
state of paramnesia, as a form of recollection. Furthermore,
the experience, unlike that of Chandos, contains a mystical
and intense awareness of self: "Discarding infinite layers,
dissolving, I become stronger and stronger: in my innermost core I am indestructible" (PIII, 41). That inviolable
self that Chandos had despaired of finding is here not only
attained, but firmly renewed and secured as well. Yet this
self, as in all experience, can be achieved only through a
dialectic that also includes self-forgetting: "In truth," as he
says, "I remember them, and in the same measure as I give
myself to this memory, I am able to forget myself"
(PIII, 40); yet, paradoxically, the powerful recollection of
the past is infused with "a breathtaking, sensual presence"
(PIII, 38), and the sudden rediscovery of the *present* self.[48]

Considering the three modes of epiphany experienced
and described by Lord Chandos, the Homecomer, and the
traveler in Greece, we can see a definite pattern emerging.
Chandos' is the most secular type of salvation, an epiphany

[47] Hofmannsthal later dramatized this same situation—where the
stranger is projected back into ancient Greece—in his *Festspiel*, *Die
Ruinen von Athen* (1924) (DIV, 479-480).

[48] It is interesting to note that another Viennese had had an
astoundingly similar experience on the Acropolis just four years
before Hofmannsthal: Freud, in his "A Disturbance of Memory on
the Acropolis" (1937), describes an experience compounded of similar paradoxical feelings of depersonalization and *déjà vu*.

whose time is the naked edge of the present and whose habitat is the object at hand. The Homecomer, on the other hand, probes deeper into the psychology of self and finds that the reality so tragically lacking in modern Germany is not that of direct experience, but one of recollected, recognized experience, of that inner, "magical realm" formed largely during the years of childhood. In his epiphanies, self-consciousness is no longer totally absent, for there is a wordless dialogue taking place between the self and the world on a level where, as he puts it, "you can be at one with yourself" (PII, 310). The ultimate depth of the personality is not fully plumbed, however, until the "Augenblicke in Griechenland," when, in the recovery of self, all past time is recovered as well. Whereas the Homecomer had discovered the true touchstone of European reality within the memories of his childhood, the traveler in Greece, in order to reach beyond the ruins, must search his memories of the world's own beginnings. The journey into the past, particularly in the case of the traveler, ultimately leads to a rediscovery of the present self. Chandos' *Nosce te ipsum*, abandoned at the onset of his crisis, is finally written by the traveler in Greece.

That Hofmannsthal envisioned the self ultimately possessing a numinous dimension is clearly written into the metaphors that he uses to describe the three epiphanies, for they reveal a progressive retreat from the tangible.[49] Chan-

---

[49] Erwin Kobel, *Hugo von Hofmannsthal* (Berlin, 1970), interprets the epiphanies in these three essays (pp. 142-200)—as indeed he does all other works of Hofmannsthal that he treats—from the standpoint of the theme of *Sein* and *Werden*. Because of his metaphysical bias, Kobel has little to say about Hofmannsthal's language, his images and metaphors, and the changing role of psychological time, i.e., memory. With little differentiation, he regards all three of the above essays by Hofmannsthal as portraying the self as "gesammeltes Dasein . . . , dem Werden nicht entfremdet und nicht dem Sein" (p. 200).

dos finds momentary surcease from surrounding chaos in "a kind of feverish thinking, but thinking in a *substance* more immediate, more fluid, more glowing than words" (PII, 19; italics mine). The metaphor is a material one, for the epiphany itself is basically immanent and secular. For the Homecomer, however, the language of the epiphany has become a language of color, one in which "the Wordless, the Everlasting, the Immense, abandon themselves, a language more exalted than sounds" (PII, 308). (Moreover, the last two letters describing this type of epiphany were actually first published separately under the title "Colors.") Yet when the traveler in Greece is granted his ultimate vision, even colors disappear and the controlling metaphor becomes one of pure light. The bright colors of impressionism[50] give way before the pure *claritas* of Neoplatonism; and amid the abstract outlines of body, mass, surface, and eyelid—the eye embodying for Hofmannsthal as for Plotinus the most spiritual of the senses (PIV, 289)—the lost, forgotten self of Chandos shines forth with the whole, bright light of a Neoplatonic essence.[51]

[50] It should be noted, however, that the Homecomer's description of Van Gogh's colors already represents an overcoming of the purely impressionistic view. Cf. his statement, "But what are colors if the innermost life of the objects doesn't break through in them!" (PII, 303) with Mach's "Thing, body, matter, are nothing apart from the combinations of the elements—the colors, sounds, and so forth— nothing apart from their so-called attributes" (pp. 6-7).

[51] The transcendence of the Greek experience for Hofmannsthal is indicated in a letter to Marie Taxis in which he speaks of the peculiar timelessness of Greece (BII, 321-322). The suggestion that colors are merely "metaphors" for a higher light is also hinted at in Hofmannsthal's journal, where he states that colors themselves are only "the means for the revelation of the light which passes through" (A, 117)—a statement that amounts to a "platonization" of impressionism.

FOUR Remembrance within Change: The Morality of the Allomatic

Jede neue bedeutende Bekanntschaft zerlegt uns und setzt uns neu zusammen.   (A, 27)

Der Sinn der Ehe ist wechselseitige Auflösung und Palingenesie.   (A, 29)

IN 1907, the same year in which he wrote "Die Briefe des Zurückgekehrten" and began work on *Andreas*, Hofmannsthal composed a short essay entitled "Furcht." Conceived as an imaginary dialogue between Laidion and Hymnis, two dancers and prostitutes, and written in the style of Lucian's anti-Platonic *Dialogues of the Courtesans*, the essay actually presents a compact treatise on the psychology of time, morality, and the Dionysian. The dialogue opens with a Greek sailor leaving Laidion with his payment of four drachmas and a captivating tale of his travels in foreign seas. His tale, set on an uncharted, paradisal island, makes such a deep impression on Laidion that she has to retell it immediately to Hymnis. It seems that once a year on this island, at a certain season, the islanders gather together to reenact a sacred, Dionysian dance, a wordless celebration of their gods of fertility and renewal. "They dance like that only once, only once a year," Laidion tells Hymnis. "The young men crouch on the ground and the girls of the island stand in front of them, all together, and their bodies are like one body, they stand so still. Then they dance, and in the end they give themselves to the youths,

60

to any youth—whoever reaches for them, they are his. They do it for the gods, and the gods bless it" (PII, 315).

In spite of Hymnis' uncomprehending comments Laidion continues to explain her deep-seated envy of the mythical islanders: namely, that she herself—whether in dance or in love—can never attain that bliss and ecstasy the natives achieve during their ritual dance; for they, unlike her and all others of the civilized world, know no anxiety. Even wishing and hoping, she says, are nothing but disguised forms of this same anxiety of the world. To Hymnis' retort that she herself is free of fear and anxiety when she dances, Laidion replies: "But you do have wishes, and wishes are anxiety. All your dancing is nothing but wishing. . . . Can you ever, even for two hours, get rid of anxiety?" (PII, 314). The essay closes with Laidion beginning to dance, in a desperate attempt to imitate the islanders and to attain their state of ecstatic transport; and yet, just as she begins to sense a touch of ecstasy she collapses, and her first words when she opens her eyes again are a bitter cry "that there is somewhere such an island where they dance and are happy without the thorn of hope. For . . . that's everything —everything, Hymnis: to be happy without hope" (PII, 319).

Hofmannsthal's essay, in its oblique fashion, makes several important points with regard to time and the psychology of anxiety, hope, and Dionysian forgetting. Perhaps the most obvious point is that the heritage of Western man, in opposition to the ritualized existence of primitives, is above all an outraged sense of temporality. Man's fall was into time, and his essence consists, in Laidion's words (and in a phrase that anticipates Heidegger in uncanny fashion), of "yearning and anxiety and desire and *Verworfenheit*" (PII, 318). Moreover, although Hofmannsthal actually uses

61

the word "Furcht" throughout the essay and as his title, it is clear from the context that what he is referring to is what Kierkegaard described in *The Concept of Dread* and what Freud, ten years after Hofmannsthal's essay, would define in his *General Introduction to Psychoanalysis* as *Angst* or anxiety: not the fear of a specific object, but rather a general state of emotional tension characterized by apprehension and fearfulness. Yet Hofmannsthal does more than presage the *memento mori* of later existentialists; he also makes the significant point that even hope itself is a mixed blessing at best, as it, too, like anxiety, can only remind us of our imprisonment in time. When we recall that hope originally belonged to the Pauline trinity of the Christian faith, and that even Schiller, in his deeply psychological poem "Resignation," had accorded hope at least the role of consoler in this world, we perceive the radical modernity of Hofmannsthal's standpoint. The function of hope has shifted from that of a psychic anodyne for the pains of existence to that of yet another goading thorn in the side of existential man.

Most important from our point of view, however, is the implicit critique in the essay of any would-be resurrection of the Dionysian in modern life; total forgetting, total loss of self, is not possible in today's world. "They are virgins," as Laidion says of the islanders, "and have forgotten it, they are supposed to become wives and mothers and have forgotten it: everything to them is ineffable. And then they dance" (PII, 318). The timelessness of the barbarian celebrants is achieved, in other words, at the expense of a loss of both memory and self. To use Nietzschean terms, the Apollonian *principium individuationis* vanishes completely in the midst of the Dionysian transport. And yet it is precisely Hofmannsthal's point that European man will never be able to revert to this state of being. The Nietzschean revival of the Dionysian side of life (which finds its latter-day counterparts in the orgasmic credo of Wilhelm Reich and in Norman O. Brown's resurrection of the Dionysian Ego) is ultimately doomed to failure, for it wills the impossible: that man renounce, together with all his anxieties, his will both to hope and to remember. Even in dance (and here again the criticism of Nietzschean vitalism is apparent) this is impossible, for, as the end of Hofmannsthal's *Elektra* demonstrates, the dance of joy, in an absolute form, becomes a dance of death.

In the figure of the dancer Laidion it is clear that we actually are viewing a later version of the adventurer-figure of Hofmannsthal's early period. In both, the attempt to thwart temporal anxiety by living in the euphoric present can only lead to eventual collapse. Man is, in Hofmannsthal's view, doomed to remember and to hope, whether he wants to or not. The Nietzschean vision of revitalizing the Dionysian must remain a fiction, an imaginary ideal. The immediate result of this is that Hofmannsthal throughout his life became ever more concerned with the moral dimension of time, in particular with the problem of reconciling ethical remembrance with the need for personal growth and change. This is, in fact, where his concept of the allomatic (*das Allomatische*) comes into play, for this important concept represents none other than Hofmannsthal's attempt to reconcile the life-style of the rememberer with that of the adventurer, to unite the inescapable fact of European morality with the alluring fiction of the island dancers.

"The allomatic principle," as Hofmannsthal informs us in *Ad me ipsum*, refers to the social and ethical process of "mutual change" ("gegenseitige Verwandlung") between two or more persons, and he adds that his own tale *Die Frau ohne Schatten* presents a "triumph of the allomatic [process]" in the form of a "social allegory" (A, 218). The word "allomatic" itself is Hofmannsthal's own neologism, a word obviously analogous to "automatic," and yet formed from the Greek *allomatos*, meaning "occurring because of *another's* influence."[52] Although it was also to play a role in *Andreas*,[53] the concept is probably best understood by referring to Hofmannsthal's libretto for *Ariadne auf Naxos*, which appeared in 1912, one year before the *Frau ohne Schatten*. Not only does Hofmannsthal cite as an example of the allomatic the figure of Bacchus from this opera (A, 218), but he also comments further on the work in a letter to Richard Strauss, published in 1912. Although the allomatic is not mentioned in the letter, it is clear from the context that it is precisely this mystic process of "mutual change" that he is intent upon describing and explaining to Strauss.

Hofmannsthal begins in the letter by touching upon what is to him life's deepest moral dilemma: the problem of reconciling the need to remember with the need to forget. Ariadne, as we recall, has been deserted on the island of Naxos by Theseus, her husband. Bacchus, on the other hand, the "fateful bridegroom" (A, 218), as Hofmannsthal calls him, has just escaped from the clutches of the sorceress Circe. The change that both of them—Ariadne in particular—must undergo in order to reconcile their sudden love for one another with their own past life is one of the opera's central themes, a theme that belongs, as Hofmannsthal explains to Strauss, to those "open secrets" of life that are more closely related to the language of music than to that

[52] See the notes to *Andreas* in Hugo von Hofmannsthal, *Selected Prose*, trans. M. Hottinger and T. & J. Stern (New York, 1952), p. 381.

[53] See Hofmannsthal's notes to *Andreas* (E, 243).

of the spoken word. Yet change, in Hofmannsthal's vocabulary, belongs to the realm of the amoral adventurer; it is "living one's life" to the full, as he puts it. "Whoever wants to live must transcend himself, must change"; in a word, "he must forget." The moral category of steadfastness and fidelity ("Beharren") on the other hand can only mean "stagnation and death." The tragic dilemma arises when we thus realize that "all human dignity is bound up with steadfastness, with not forgetting, with faithfulness" (PIII, 138).

"This," Hofmannsthal concludes, "is one of the abyss-like contradictions upon which life is built, like the Delphic temple over its bottomless split in the earth. It has been pointed out to me that I have not ceased wondering my whole life long about the eternal secret of this contradiction. Thus Ariadne here is paired off once more against Zerbinetta [the coquettish dancer who was to star in the epilogue 'Die ungetreue Zerbinetta und ihre vier Liebhaber,' but who now, in a touch of romantic irony, is to play in the opera *Ariadne* itself instead], just as Electra once stood opposite Chrysothemis. Chrysothemis wanted to live, nothing more; and she knew that whoever wants to live, must forget. Electra doesn't forget" (PIII, 138-139). With these words, Hofmannsthal has circumscribed the entire problem of the allomatic process, for Ariadne, the princess who "could be the wife of only *one* man, could be abandoned by only *one* man" (PIII, 139; Hofmannsthal's italics), has indeed become the wife of a second husband, just as Bacchus himself, who yesterday was only a child, has fled from the arms of Circe to those of his second lover, Ariadne (PIII, 141). The transformation in each, occurring as it does through another's influence, cannot be condemned as an immoral one; it must be termed, in Hofmannsthal's word, allomatic.

Actually, the question of the allomatic process connects

with a much larger problem in Hofmannsthal, one which, if we examine it for a moment, may help us to see the concept of the allomatic in a wider perspective. This problem, briefly stated, is one of opposites. We need only cast a quick glance at any of Hofmannsthal's works to realize that he was fascinated, almost compulsively so, with all the polarities and contradictions of human existence. His writing, from its recurrent motifs of night and day, present and past, and height and depth, to its most finely calculated oxymoronic phrase, is informed throughout by a powerful and yet subtle design of antinomies. The pattern is most apparent in his notebooks, where the artistic will often asserts itself in a blatantly schematic manner: "Of the antinomies of life, one or the other becomes the axis of our spiritual existence" (A, 227), he writes, and again, as late as two years before his death: "Poet. Central this: counterbalance —the harmonic feeling in antithesis—to unite—dual significance—night and day—stagnation and creation—historical and unhistorical—to balance being and becoming—also rich and poor—present and past—to value and devalue words—even the counterbalance of the exact with the inexact" (A, 208). Life itself for Hofmannsthal was a "complete unification of that which cannot be unified" (A, 200), and the supreme task of the poet was to attempt precisely this unification; the subtitle of *Andreas*—"Die Vereinigten"—for instance, points figuratively in the same direction.

Merely to document this dualistic bias of Hofmannsthal's mind would bring us little reward. Such diverse writers as Hölderlin (cf. [A, 208]), Goethe, Yeats, Broch, Hesse, and Thomas Mann have also been fascinated by mystic and non-mystic resolutions of polarities and antinomies in their works, as have undoubtedly many other writers. What makes Hofmannsthal's case both unique and fruitful, however (and this is where the allomatic applies), is that practically all of his opposites derive from two primal pairs, one temporal and one spatial: "Two antinomies were to be resolved," he notes, "that of passing time and duration—and that of loneliness and the community" (A, 228). Moreover, the primal pairs are actually parallel to one another, for the relationship of the individual to the community is merely the spatial analogue of the present moment's relationship to a duration of moments extending into the past. This is a lesson learned by both Andrea and Claudio, as we have already seen; for in each of them the sudden awareness of the past is triggered by an equally abrupt awareness of an ethical connection with others in space. The polarities of the individual and the community, of time (in the sense of fleeting, disparate moments) and duration (in the sense of a continuity of moments extending into the past), are thus moral ones, and it is in a moral sense that the allomatic process would reconcile both pairs of opposites—change with duration, and the individual with others.

At the risk of being over-schematic, we might arrange Hofmannsthal's design of polarities as follows:

FORGETTING	REMEMBERING
Unfaithfulness	Faithfulness (*Treue*)
Change (*Verwandlung*)	Steadfastness (*Beharren*)
Zerbinetta	Adriadne
Harlequin	Bacchus
Chrysothemis	Electra
Impressionistic flux (*vergehende Zeit*)	Temporal duration (*Dauer*)
Einsamkeit	*Gemeinsamkeit*
The Adventurer	The Married Man
The Aesthetic	The Ethical

67

Zufall	*Schicksal*
Präexistenz	*Existenz*
The *Glück* of the	Laidion's *Hoffnung* and
island dancers	*Furcht*

Das Allomatische
gegenseitige Verwandlung, or
remembrance within change

The allomatic process, in which ethical relations are preserved in spite of personal change and growth, not only
connects the two major antinomies of Hofmannsthal's
thought, but also, as we shall see in the next chapter, forms
the basis of his concept of Bildung. For the "delphic abyss"
between personal development and faithfulness is precisely
that which, in Hofmannsthal's Bildungsroman, underlies
Andreas' deep uncertainties with regard to Romana and
which is mirrored in the split personality of Maria-
Mariquita in Venice.[54]

What, then, do we see in Hofmannsthal's concept of the
allomatic process beyond an esoteric term for the mystic
synthesis of remembrance and change necessary to all
moral Bildung? First of all, to glance backward in time for
a moment, it distinguishes Hofmannsthal's temporal concept from that of a writer whose works exercised an im-

[54] Alewyn, who has excellent remarks in his essay on *Andreas* on
the polarized personalities in Hofmannsthal's works, is less concerned
with the specific categories of time, memory, and morality than with
demonstrating that from the time of *Andreas* onward (ca. 1912),
Hofmannsthal's pieces tended more and more to center on a quartet
of characters rather than a trio, thereby transforming the latent
tragic ending into the traditional "comic" ending of marriage. See
Über Hugo von Hofmannsthal, pp. 152-158, in particular his closing
remark that "Die Figur des magischen Quadrats . . . ist die äussere
Gestalt jenes sittlichen Vorgangs der gegenseitigen Verwandlung,
den Hofmannsthal in der Geheimsprache des *Ad me ipsum* als die
allomatische Lösung bezeichnete" (p. 158).

mense influence upon him throughout his entire life—from the concept of time in Goethe. This point is important, for it has become a commonplace among some Hofmannsthal critics to compare Hofmannsthal's intense concern for spiritual resolutions and humanistic harmonies with similar concerns in Goethe. If we read carefully, however, we see important and instructive differences between the two writers. One of the greatest of these is the fact that in Goethe most ideas of change, development, metamorphosis, and Bildung are formulated in a language whose central metaphors have been taken from the organic and botanical realm, one in which there is notably no memory and thus no problems of growth and change resulting in a series of moral mishaps and tragic discontinuities.

In the poem "Dauer im Wechsel" (1804), for instance—in which Emil Staiger perceives the essence and epitome of Goethe's concept of time[55]—the dangers of ethical vacillation inherent in a philosophy of constant growth and change are merely touched upon in one line:

> Weggeschwunden ist die Lippe,
> Die im Kusse sonst genas,

and a cluster of life-embodying organic metaphors effectively obscures the inherent moral ambiguity of the entire process:

> Gleich mit jedem Regengusse
> Ändert sich dein holdes Tal.

Unlike the human soul, nature tolerates no jumps or gaps— *natura non facit saltus*—and Goethe's emphasis on organic growth and the unceasing creation of new forms, as in "Eins und Alles" (1823),

---

[55] Emil Staiger, *Die Zeit als Einbildungskraft des Dichters* (Zürich, 1963), pp. 109-160.

69

> Es soll sich regen, schaffend handeln,
> Erst sich gestalten, dann verwandeln,

necessarily leads to a total devaluation of an ethic of stead-fastness and constancy (*Beharren* and *Treue* in Hofmanns-thal's sense):

> Denn alles muss in Nichts zerfallen,
> Wenn es im Sein beharren will.

Hofmannsthal's own insight into the importance of remain-ing steadfast in human relationships represents a major de-parture from the Goethean concept of time.[56]

On the other hand, looking ahead in time, the concept of the allomatic process separates Hofmannsthal from a great number of modern writers as well. Unlike such authors as Proust, Rilke, Joyce, and Mann, who are largely concerned with seeking out "timeless" realms of human experience and with creating temporal stases within their works in order to refute time's flow, Hofmannsthal is much more con-cerned with the tragic situations that arise when one admits that time, with its ineluctable dimensions of hoping and remembering, is an inescapable fact of life, no matter how much one may theorize about transcending it. The myth of the timeless Dionysian dancers must remain a myth. The stuff of consciousness, for Hofmannsthal, is the before and

---

[56] The amoral adventurer who appears in Hofmannsthal's dramas, as well as in those of many of his Viennese contemporaries (e.g., Schnitzler's *Anatol*), can be seen as the *fin de siècle* descendant of just this Goethean urge for movement, action, change, and growth. Hermann Bahr points specifically to this source for the theme: "This 'die-and-be-reborn' theme of Goethe's that we cannot develop without also steadily destroying ourselves, has become so familiar to us that if any one of us actually now thinks back only ten years, he can scarcely remember what he was like then. We are all actors and . . . all life is change." (*Dialog vom Tragischem*, pp. 71-72). Claudio, like the other young adventurers in Hofmannsthal, is the decadent great-grandson of Faust.

after of the event, and any attempt to strip time of these dimensions, to live like the dancer, the adventurer, the actor, or the aesthete in the total oblivion of the blissful present, leads to a totally amoral existence; the island girls, we recall, "give themselves . . . to any youth—whoever reaches for them" (PII, 315).

Memory remains the central concept in Hofmannsthal's view of time and change. Hofmannsthal's unflagging awareness of time's moral dimension—represented in the allomatic process—separates him not only from the organic intuition of time in Goethe, but also from the existentialist's stress on the sheer temporality of the moment, and from the modern mythographer's invocation of the timeless archetype. Ethical or allomatic commitment presupposes the ability to remember and a constant consciousness of the past.

FIVE   The Synthesis: Bildung as Vertical Time

> In der Gegenwart, die uns umgibt, ist nicht weniger Fik-
> tives als in der Vergangenheit, deren Abspiegelung wir
> Geschichte nennen. Indem wir das eine Fiktive durch das
> andere interpretieren, entsteht erst etwas, das der Mühe
> wert ist.   (A, 36)

IT WAS IN the years spanned by his two major periods of work on *Andreas*, 1907 and 1912, that Hofmannsthal's ideas on a Bildung for the individual finally reached their most mature and convincing form. Logically enough, Hofmannsthal's concept of Bildung is based upon his view of time. As we have already noted, the experience of time, in Hofmannsthal's eyes, assumed one of two archetypal patterns: either that of the Neoplatonic poet, escaping through his magic looking-glass into the vast reaches of the past, or that of the aesthetic adventurer, voyaging precariously upon the shallow wave of the present.

Hofmannsthal's bifurcation of the time-sense into remembering and forgetting might at first appear less than original. For most modern theorizers on time—much like Samuel Beckett, who defined time as the "double-headed monster of damnation and salvation"[57]—have been drawn to a dualistic view. The distinction, as William Barrett has described it, "has been expressed variously as that between clock-time and real duration (Bergson); between actual becoming as the radically discontinuous emergence of events and the continuum of time as mere

[57] Samuel Beckett, *Proust* (New York, 1931), p. 1.

72

mathematical possibility (Whitehead); between primordial temporality and the 'vulgar' understanding of time (Heidegger). There is also the common distinction between cosmic and human time; or, in its most crude formulation, between psychological and physical time."[58] What distinguishes Hofmannsthal's concept of time from such views, however, is the fact that it does not represent a mere polemic against the tyranny of technology, with its one-dimensional clocktime of Newtonian mechanics (variously associated above with "physical," "vulgar," and "mathematical" time). Hofmannsthal's heroes—unlike Kafka's harried protagonist in the anecdote "Give It Up!" who is pursued through strange city streets by the shadow of public time registered on the tower clock—are little concerned with calendars and chronometers. Hofmannsthal's two basic modes of experiencing time constitute rather a differentiation *within* the one inner, psychological time.

It is upon both of these inner dimensions of time that Hofmannsthal's concept of Bildung is predicated. For if many of the early poems and plays deal with the ironic oscillation between the two extremes of remembering and forgetting, the essays and works of the middle period present a conscious quest for a dynamic synthesis of the two in the name of Bildung. A dual consciousness—of the poet's past as well as of the adventurer's present—informs Hofmannsthal's vision of true self-development, a consciousness that would combine the recollected self and the remembrance of others (the allomatic) with a constant openness to new experience. Ideally the process combines moral loyalty with dynamic, creative growth, the two dimensions of life that are separated, as Hofmannsthal puts it in the "Adriadne" essay, by the delphic abyss of existence.

[58] William Barrett, "The Flow of Time," in *The Philosophy of Time*, ed. Richard M. Gale (Garden City, N.Y., 1967), p. 354.

This dual time sense of Bildung, as joining a sense of the past with a sense of the present, is eloquently formulated in a lecture Hofmannsthal delivered in several cities in Germany in 1906, when he was thirty-two years old. Not only the choice of the public lecture as a means of communication, but also the title of the talk—"Der Dichter und diese Zeit"—indicates the topic foremost in Hofmannsthal's mind at the time, the reconciliation of the artist with the public, of the poet with the reader. Hofmannsthal begins the talk by asserting that the distinction between the poet and the non-poet appears to him to be a totally specious one; the common reader carries within him a "fabric woven of recollected images" (PII, 231) and in certain moments can become, much like the artist, a "conqueror of time," for he is "conscious of carrying time [in the sense of both time and the times in which he lives] within him," of feeling "past and future merge in an endless present" (PII, 257-258). The reader, in effect, is granted the timeless vision that in earlier years had belonged to the poet alone, and the work of art, no longer functioning merely as an aesthetic mirror, becomes, in Hofmannsthal's eyes, an extension of life itself, "since literature is nothing other than the work of the living" (PII, 256).

The poet, on the other hand, is in a sense the same as before: "the dead live within him"; he "can never . . . forget anything completely" (PII, 246). Yet an important change has taken place, for his exclusive province of the past has now expanded to include the present as well. The point is stressed by Hofmannsthal again and again: the poet "combines the elements of the age within himself. The present is in him or nowhere else . . . he creates the world of connections . . . between past and present . . . dream and thing" (PII, 245). The poet, in a word, now exists in the "house of this time . . . of this present, of this reality" (PII, 244). Past

time is no longer represented as a weightless, hermetic
world of magic mirrors, caves, and crystalline rivers (as in
Falun), but as an immense weight pressing upon the poet's
shoulders in the here and now; he lives "under the pressure
of immeasurable atmospheres, like the diver in the depths
of the sea" (PII, 248), "under a pressure like that of the entire ocean . . . illuminated by no light, not even by a small
miner's lamp" (PII, 252). To put it in the characteristic
imagery of "Reiselied," Hofmannsthal now no longer sees
the magic wall of the garden well as *dividing* the catas-
trophic present from the serene, quasi-eternal depths of the
past, but rather as *connecting* the two.

Hofmannsthal's move towards this synthesis of poet and
public, past and present, did not, of course, occur suddenly
in the years 1906 and 1907, although these years were obviously decisive with regard to his plans for writing a Bildungsroman (whose hero, typically enough, combines
qualities of both poet and non-poet). Like many of Hofmannsthal's ethical ideas, that of the poet as being related
to others in both time and space is evident in his poetry
from a very early date. When in his lecture, for instance, he
suggests that the "living fire from stars long since consumed
by icy space" (PII, 245) can still reach and touch the "lidless
eye" (PII, 244) of the poet, he is merely quoting his own
poetry of some ten years before:

> Ganz vergessener Völker Müdigkeiten
> Kann ich nicht abtun von meinen Lidern,
> Noch weghalten von der erschrockenen Seele
> Stummes Niederfallen ferner Sterne.   (G, 19)

And when he furthermore asserts that for the poet the
"present is interwoven in indescribable fashion with the
past," that "in the pores of his body he senses what has
come down to him ['das Herübergelebte'] from past days,

75

from distant fathers and patriarchs never known, from vanished peoples, closed epochs" (PII, 245), he is again quoting from an early poem:

> Dann: das ich auch vor hundert Jahren war
> Und meine Ahnen, die im Totenhemd,
> Mit mir verwandt sind wie mein eignes Haar,
>
> So eins mit mir als wie mein eignes Haar.
>
> (G, 17)

As Hofmannsthal explains in an early letter (with a touch of Kantian terminology), the goal of the artist is not to flee to a dream-like land of the past, but "to multiply the present by assimilating the lives of others and by living the present to the full, through reflection, through recalling the past. For since time is something highly relative, a mere perceptual category of the mind, one can actually fill a moment with infinite meaning" (BI, 148).

What we have referred to in the title of this chapter as "vertical time" is none other than this very same ideal: the constant infusion of present experience with the spirit of the past. As stated in our epigraph, life's truth, its inmost essence, can only emerge when the fictive present is confronted by and interpreted through the fictive past. Through the act of constant interpretation we come to know the values of life, and we also grow. Yet why term this dual time sense a "vertical" one? Several possible answers present themselves. The metaphor is perhaps best explained theoretically by William James, who in his *Principles of Psychology* hits precisely on what Hofmannsthal had in mind: "If we represent the actual time-stream of our thinking by an horizontal line, the thought *of* the stream or of any segment of its length, past, present, or to come, might be figured in a perpendicular raised upon the horizontal at a certain point."[59] Other critics have similarly pointed to the (at least psychological) validity of envisioning the past as spatially behind and beneath us.[60] Practically speaking, however, we already possess an explanation for Hofmannsthal's use of this metaphor from our explorations into the time imagery of the early works; the characteristic images of looking-glass, eye, well, lake, and cavern all point to a depth-dimension in experience that Hofmannsthal consistently equates with past time. Vertical time, in short, becomes Hofmannsthal's term for a consciousness of this constantly accumulating "depth" of the past behind and beneath us.

This concept of the past as the infinite ground of the present is an idea inherent in many of Hofmannsthal's works, even before 1906. In most cases it is furthermore associated, in a tradition perhaps more Austrian than German, with the feeling of a mystical kinship with ancestors. The grandmother's statement in *Falun*, for instance: "And how the dead stir within me today!" (G, 459); the image of a young girl staring into an old mirror found in a forgotten trunk and discovering the reflection, not of herself, but of her ancestor (PII, 377); the "accumulated strength of the line of ancestors within us," the "layers of amassed, collective memory" that Hofmannsthal invokes, in another essay, in speaking of coming to terms with the "thousandfold phantoms from the past"; and the lone voice of the last member of the Contarin family, asserting that "we are reflections of our ancestors," that we are actually "still the same ones, only older," and that this difference in age is what affords us our "spiritual coordinates" (E, 95)—all of these in-

[59] William James, *The Principles of Psychology*, Chapter 15.
[60] Paul Fraisse, *The Psychology of Time* (New York, 1963), p. 284.

stances attest to the fact that Hofmannsthal viewed the present moment, no matter how fascinating it might be, as but the top-most, visible point of the vast, unseen pyramid of the past.

In one instance, however, and that fairly late in his life, Hofmannsthal actually uses the word "vertical" for this time sense. It occurs in his introduction to Brecht's drama *Baal*, a play to which Hofmannsthal was not sympathetic, but that he clearly sensed as being symptomatic of the intellectual climate of the time. *Baal*, in his eyes, heralded the advent of the new mass man, of the man who was fast abandoning the Apollonian heights of classical humanism for the twentieth-century's Dionysian arena of "blood, creature, thing" (LIV, 415). In Hofmannsthal's prologue (1926), written in the form of a dialogue, the youthful actor Homolka, who will play the role of Baal, chastises the actor Thimig (in part a spokesman for some of Hofmannsthal's own ideas) for his "reactionary" Viennese faith in his cultural and ancestral legacy:

> HOMOLKA: Herr Thimig, as long as you continue to think vertically to such a degree, we can't understand one another.
>
> THIMIG: I think vertically?
>
> FRIEDELL: Yes, that's the impression I've also had. It's a sickness in the Viennese air.
>
> HOMOLKA: You think in generations of ancestors, and you put yourself at the end. The new man thinks horizontally. In the cross-section of the present. We don't descend from anyone.   (LIV, 416)

The present age, they inform Thimig, is desperately in need of "redemption" from the intolerable burden that has been thrust upon it—that of selfhood and self-development. "Individuality," Homolka says to Thimig, "is one of the arabesques that we have cast aside," and Friedell adds that the self, an "offspring of the sixteenth century that the nineteenth century had fattened up to size," is now a thing of the past; since 1914 in particular we have witnessed the virtual burial of that "weary concept . . . the European Individual" (LIV, 419). "Reactionary" vertical time is thus the time sense of Bildung—of European Individualism, as Friedell and Homolka put it.

In this dialogue we have not only a definition of vertical time (as life's recollected dimension), but also an important reason why Hofmannsthal gradually came to this view of time. He consciously set vertical time against horizontal time, against the continual forgetting of the masses. "It's a question," Thimig finally admits, "of whether or not the confined self of the individual still exists for the horizontally thinking man of today" (LIV, 421). Shorn of his past—be it private, ancestral, or communal—modern man escapes all defining differences, and thus the European individual passes painlessly (and mindlessly) into the anonymous community of European mass man. The experience of the first World War in particular, Hofmannsthal implies, contributed in numerous ways to this mass jettisoning of the past and the almost compulsive turning to things of the moment, to the here and now of all that was modern and contemporary. This cultural, or anticultural, climate was perhaps best described—seven years before the war—by the *Zurückgekehrter* who, much like Friedell at the end of the *Baal* Prologue, fears that the ground may literally be giving way beneath him (PII, 280). A man whose reading-matter abroad had included such novels as *Wilhelm Meister*, he returns to Europe only to be pursued by a shallow, fragmented feeling of the present (PII, 279, 289): the Germans, he finds, with their idealism, their humanism, their taverns, their statues of Arminius, are heedlessly engaged in such projects as "pulling Charlemagne from his grave in order to photograph the cloth wound around his bones" and are eagerly "converting their sacred cathedrals into beer halls" (PII, 291). A godless view of the past predominates everywhere.

Several factors, in Hofmannsthal's view, were contributing to this fanatic levelling of man's temporal coordinates to the protean absurdities of the present. The decline of religion was one obvious cause: from a vertical framework of eternity in the Middle Ages to one of mere history (or evolution or progress) in the nineteenth century, man was now fast approaching a horizon bounded entirely by the present moment, by the space at hand; the concern for history was becoming a fascination with geography. Hofmannsthal points to the "planetary" claims of Walt Whitman, for example, as being symptomatic of this mass movement of horizontal man, and opposes it to the "actual fate of the artist," which is to sense himself as the "expression of a plurality leading back into the distant past" (A, 299). This reduction of vertical time to horizontal space was more than a literary parallel, within the *Zeitgeist*, to the Einsteinian discovery that time was but a sub-dimension of space. In sociological terms it was a direct result of the cultural fragmentation and accelerated pace of the industrial age.[61] Communication and transportation in space were effectively and ironically reducing man's mobility in time. The "once upon a time" of folk tales and histories was being replaced by the hectic "yesterday" of the worker's daily paper (PII, 292), and, we might add, was soon to be succeeded by the instantaneous "now" of the television. Even mobility itself, Hofmannsthal points out—the act of journeying—is no longer the sentimental art that it was in the days of Rousseau and Sterne, when one still had time

[61] Fraisse, pp. 169-170.

enough "to become melancholic at the sight of a dead donkey in the road" or "to pluck the fruit from trees as one passed" (PI, 77-78).

This seemingly perverse will of the common man to adhere to the hectic horizon of the moment had, however, yet a third cause, beyond that of the demise of the religious imagination and the advent of technology: very simply, this was the fact of the ever increasing amount, or depth, of the past that had to be recollected. "The single man," as Hofmannsthal remarks in a note, "took part as a child in the memories of his grandparents, and as an old man takes part in the hopes of his grandson; he spans five generations or 100 to 120 years" (A, 9-10). In addition to this span of a century in which the individual must come to feel at home is the expanse of the collective past, and in this last respect Hofmannsthal seems to have possessed a unique view of history. For unlike so many modern writers from Nietzsche to Joyce who have invoked the timeless archetypes of humanity through the myth of the eternal recurrence or of the Viconian cycle, and unlike the existentialists with their antihistoricist paeans to the reality of the present, Hofmannsthal saw history as a straight line, as a nonrepeating, accumulating series of events.

This conception of history emerges from various notes in his journals and essays. The remark of the last Contarin we have already noted, namely that we are actually "still the same ones" as our ancestors, "only older" (E, 95). Elsewhere, in his notebooks, Hofmannsthal jots down the idea of "amassing all the past once more as a pyramid of life," as well as the thought that the "problem of time" is nothing other than the problem of the "space of the spirit" ("geistiger Lebensraum") (A, 204). In his notes for *Andreas* he comments that Sacramozo, who is deeply impressed by the idea of the pyramid of life, assumes that "everything that happens later relates to all earlier events—in all directions" (E, 214-215). Carl J. Burckhardt, one of Hofmannsthal's good friends in later years, has pointed out that Hofmannsthal's view of time was very much like that of Lao-tse, who understood "that the son—in the sense of world time, the growth of mankind—is older than the father and therefore stands a step closer to the temptation to withdraw himself from the obligating past," and he goes on to say that Hofmannsthal "had a horror of forgetting the secret" contained in past traditions.[62] We need not reach to the wisdom of the East, however, for a historical analogy to Hofmannsthal's vision of world time; Francis Bacon voices a very similar sentiment in his *Novum Organum*—that it is the "old age and increasing years of the world," not the epoch of the Greeks and Romans, that "should in reality be considered as antiquity," adding with a characteristic touch of enlightened optimism that "we have reason to expect much greater things of our own age than from antiquity, since the world has grown older."[63] That Hofmannsthal was familiar with this statement seems probable for two reasons: not only did he make Bacon the recipient of the Chandos letter, but he also makes the following comment to Leopold von Andrian in a letter of the following year: "Last August I often leafed through Bacon's essays . . . [and] dreamed myself into the way these people of the sixteenth century experienced antiquity" (BI, 100).

Hofmannsthal's campaign for a creative remembrance in poet as well as non-poet is not a unique phenomenon in this century. Countless other voices as well have been raised against the shallow cult of modernism. Nietzsche's "untimely meditations" on the German *Bildungsphilister*, Hesse satirizing the Age of the Feuilleton, T. S. Eliot poetically

[62] Burckhardt, "Erinnerung an Hofmannsthal," p. 133.
[63] Book I, Section 84.

shoring his ruins in a spiritual Waste Land, Ortega y Gasset condemning the revolt of the unhistorical masses, Heidegger directing jeremiads against our second Fall into the Prosaic Age, and Aldous Huxley dismally heralding in the Age of the New Stupid—these are only a few of numerous examples. The counterplea for humanistic remembrance, particularly of literary traditions, has also taken many forms: the critic Van Wyck Brooks stressed America's need for finding a "usable past"; Eliot advanced a plea for a restored sense of literary "tradition"; E. R. Curtius emphasized that "there is nothing more pressing than to restore 'memory'" in the sense of a European cultural tradition;[64] and Northrop Frye has stated that the "culture of the past is not only the memory of mankind, but our own buried life, and the study of it leads to a recognition scene, a discovery in which we see, not our past lives, but the total cultural form of our present life." And in a sentence that could equally well have come from Hofmannsthal, he concludes that it is not only the "poet but his reader who is subject to the obligation to 'make it new.' "[65] Finally, W. H. Auden has added his voice in a prayer to the Muse of History, that she may "teach us our recollections."[66]

[64] Ernst Robert Curtius, *European Literature and the Latin Middle Ages*, trans. W. R. Trask (Princeton, 1953), pp. 395-397.

[65] Northrop Frye, *Anatomy of Criticism* (Princeton, 1957), p. 346.

[66] See W. H. Auden's "Homage to Clio." It should perhaps be mentioned at this point that the problems touched upon here, particularly that involving the steady cultural amnesia of the masses, may very well connect with what Mircea Eliade has described as the "Terror of History," the aversion of modern man to the dismal linearity of time and to the ever-accumulating burden of historical self-consciousness, be this private or political; see the last chapter of his *Cosmos and History* (New York, 1959). For further interesting observations on this important topic, see W. J. Bate, *The Burden of the Past and the English Poet* (Cambridge, Mass., 1970), and John

Hofmannsthal's own plea for an awakened sense of vertical time, in the sense of a revitalized *Kulturpolitik*, becomes most central in his postwar writings. In the well-known speech, "Das Schrifttum als geistiger Raum der Nation" (1927), for example, his appeal is for an act of collective remembrance, for a Bildung that is national in scope: no longer must only the whole man learn to move together, but the entire population as well. In the speech he denounces the fragmentation both on the "plane of simultaneity" and in the "depth of generation-succession" (PIV, 395) and advances a plea for a reunification of the two—of the present with the depth of the past, of everyday life with its buried literary traditions, of *Realpolitik* with *Kultur*, of *Nation* with *Schrifttum*. The key terms in the synthesis, rhetorically speaking, are the oxymoronic metaphors "geistiger Raum" and "konservative Revolution"—the latter being the celebrated solution that he invokes at the end of the speech. The former phrase, the virtually untranslatable concept of the "spiritual landscape," suggests the ideal realm in which political action would merge with cultural meditation and remembrance; it is the domain in which the "Bildung of a true nation" must eventually take place (PIV, 412).[67] With the latter phrase, Hofmannsthal was again attempting to articulate the concept we have termed vertical time; for the "conservative revolution," as Carl Burckhardt has pointed out, was above all a "protest against that fatal forgetting which would abandon everything to the present moment."[68] What represented, in political terms, the merging of a cultural traditionalism with an economic socialism becomes,

---

Lukacs, *Historical Consciousness or the Remembered Past* (New York, 1968).

[67] See also (A, 204) to the effect that the concept of the "spiritual landscape" actually refers to a problem of time.

[68] Burckhardt, "Erinnerung an Hofmannsthal," pp. 148-149.

in the vocabulary of time, the uniting of remembrance with both change and forgetting—precisely Hofmannsthal's formula for *private* Bildung.

Yet there resides in these postwar pleas a very real danger as well, namely, the danger of abstractionism. For the call to Bildung, when issued to the public at large rather than to the private individual, tends to become vague and rhetorical. In fact, the metaphors Hofmannsthal employs in later years to articulate the ideal of vertical time become so general as to blur the message itself. In his notebooks, for example, he equates vertical time ("die Generationskette") with the timeless aspects of the super-ego, and thus with something between Freud's memory traces and Jung's collective unconscious. The three figures associated in the note with this phenomenon—the magician of the "Traum von grosser Magie," the Madman of the *Kleines Welttheater*, and the miner of *Falun*—all point to the fact, incidentally, that Hofmannsthal's ideal of ethical remembrance grew directly out of the experiences with Neoplatonic recollection during his lyric decade (A, 226).[69] In the essays, moreover, he even uses the idea of pure, unreflected light to express vertical time: just as water images in the earlier works had embodied for him the timeless, ageless quality of the past, now light, a far more abstract metaphor, serves the same purpose (PIV, 154); what had been merely a subordinate dimension of the earlier metaphor—the light reflected in wells and rivers—is now used independently to symbolize remembrance. Similarly, in the late essay "Erinnerung," memory becomes an abstract, spiritual landscape, very similar to that described in the later speech; a dreamlike realm of mirror images, it is also characterized by a marvelous light (PIV, 204).

Perhaps the most striking example, however, occurs in

[69] See also in this connection (A, 219).

Hofmannsthal's introductory piece to an anthology of essays on language. Here remembrance is equated directly with the phenomenon of language itself; in the act of speaking, Hofmannsthal explains, man "acknowledges himself as a creature who can never forget." With this statement, however, together with its corrollary that there thus exists a "power of the *Volksgemeinschaft* over the single individual" (PIV, 439), Hofmannsthal ironically brings his humanization of poetic memory to a form of *reductio ad absurdum*. For as the National Socialists would demonstrate six short years later, language, when divorced from the individual conscience, particularly that of the writer, can become the direct tool of *de*humanization. To imply, even rhetorically, that language at large was the true measure and repository of memory was, ethically speaking, as disastrous and untenable a pronouncement as the assertion in the earlier years that the sole touchstone of memory was the magic word of the poet.

It may be helpful at this point if we stand back from Hofmannsthal for a moment and, observing his ideas on time and memory from a more distant remove, sharpen our focus through a brief comparison with several other writers. The name that first comes to mind when the topic of memory in literature arises is undoubtedly that of Marcel Proust, and there are indeed several interesting parallels between him and Hofmannsthal. Proust, like Hofmannsthal, was concerned with the idea that the past may somehow redeem us from the barren present; furthermore, both writers also rejected the comforting belief in any cyclical pattern of events, for they viewed history as a non-reversible, rectilinear process. They also shared certain qualities of the disposition normally attributed to the mystic: an awareness of an underlying duality in the world, a sense of the reality of the unseen, and a visionary, almost eidetic susceptibility to images recalled from memory. In each writer, however, the basic disposition underwent a decidedly different interpretation: whereas Hofmannsthal continually stressed the activity of interpreting the remembered images in the light of the present (as in the epigraph to this section), Proust, in giving himself over to the "magic lantern" of memory, essentially assumed the passive stance of the mystic. The act of remembrance for Proust was totally "involuntary" and performed for him, as Georges Poulet has pointed out, much the same function as involuntary grace does in Christian thought. Stressing the timelessness of the remembered image, its utter divorce from the common world of the senses, Proust surrendered himself completely to Neoplatonic despair over the transient insufficiency of the concrete world: "How paradoxical it is," he writes at the end of *Swann's Way*, "to seek in reality for the pictures that are stored in one's memory, which must inevitably lose the charm that comes to them from memory itself and from their not being apprehended by the senses."[70] Whereas Hofmannsthal assigns to recollection a voluntary, ethical side (the allomatic), Proust, in the end, can only express his eloquent despair over the fact that the "remembrance of a particular form is but regret for a particular moment; and houses, roads, avenues are as fugitive, alas, as the years."

One might add in passing that Henri Bergson (whose proverbial influence on Proust has been convincingly refuted by Georges Poulet),[71] has theorized on the psychology of memory in a fashion amazingly similar to that of Hofmannsthal. (Hofmannsthal's library, it is interesting to note, contained two editions of Bergson's *Matter and*

[70] Marcel Proust, *Swann's Way*, trans. C. K. Scott Moncrieff (New York, Modern Library), p. 611.

[71] See the chapter on Proust in *Studies in Human Time* (Baltimore, 1956).

Memory—a German edition of 1908 and a French one of 1910.)[72] The most important parallel between Bergson and Hofmannsthal lies in their common vision of memory as the long-lost link between all dualisms, both physical and metaphysical: memory, Bergson states, represents precisely the "intersection of mind and matter." Moreover, by blurring the boundaries between perception and recollection, he is able to employ the word "image" to demolish all Cartesian and Kantian dualisms. For image connotes for him an existence *between* the "mind" of the idealist and the realist's "matter"; it is an "existence placed halfway between the 'thing' and the 'representation'" (a statement that, in a fascinating parallel, places Bergson's "images" very close to what Ernst Mach termed "sensations"). Furthermore, memories for Bergson, as he explains elsewhere, form at any given moment a "solid whole, a pyramid, so to speak, whose point is inserted precisely into our present action. . . . Yes, I believe indeed that all our past life is there, preserved even to the most infinitesimal details, and that we forget nothing, and that all that we have felt, perceived, thought, willed, from the first awakening of our consciousness, survives indestructibly."[73] This was precisely Hofmannsthal's view as well.

Another philosopher with whom Hofmannsthal bears a surprising kinship, one whose metaphysics are far more abstract than those of Bergson, is Martin Heidegger. Although Heidegger's special emphasis on the future tense and death and his complex notion of existential time as a co-presence of the three mystical "ex-tases" of past-present-future are not part of Hofmannsthal's thought, his reflec-

[72] See Michael Hamburger, "Hofmannsthals Bibliothek," *Euphorion*, 55 (1961), 28.

[73] Henri Bergson, *Matter and Memory*, trans. N. M. Paul and W. S. Palmer (Garden City, N.Y., 1959), pp. xv, xi, and 33.

tions on memory do bear a close resemblance to those of the poet. For Being, life's highest goal for Heidegger (and the hidden godhead of his metaphysics), is to be reached largely through a process of recollection, just as it had been lost at the time of the Greeks through "forgetting." (This prescribed process of recollection is mimed, moreover, by the etymological reminiscences inherent in Heidegger's own idiosyncratic style.) Heidegger's "Being, unlike a triangle," as William Barrett has demonstrated, "is something of which we can have no mental picture or representation. We reach it by a kind of thought other than conceptual reason. 'Think,' and 'thank' are kindred roots, and the German word *an-denken*—literally, 'to think on'—means to remember; hence, for Heidegger, think, thank, and remember are kindred notions.[74] Real thinking, thinking that is rooted in Being, is at once an act of thanking and remembrance. When a dear friend says, in parting, 'Think of me!' this does not mean 'Have a mental picture of me!' but: 'Let me (even in my absence) be present with you.' " Not only does this "thinking that recalls" appear to have ethical implications (as does, for instance, Hofmannsthal's notion of the allomatic), but it would also view the act of forgetting as a form of spiritual loss. In Barrett's words, if we choose to forget Being, "then all our human and humanistic enterprises are threatened with the void, since our existence itself would thereby be torn from its root."[75]

According to Heidegger, then, our task is not only to face up to the fact of our own death (the existentialist emphasis on our radical finiteness), but also, as heirs of the past, to appropriate our heritage as a form of internal, subjective

[74] See Heidegger's preface, which he wrote in 1949, to his 1929 lecture "Was ist Metaphysik?" (translated by Walter Kaufmann in *Existentialism from Dostoevsky to Sartre* [Cleveland, 1963]).

[75] William Barrett, *Irrational Man* (Garden City, N.Y., 1962), p. 235.

history, one which he calls "historicality." As he describes it in *Being and Time* (1927), this process must be an authentic one, "in which Being *hands* itself *down* to itself, free for death, in a possibility which it has inherited and yet has chosen." The process of recollecting, as in Hofmannsthal, is the burden of the individual, and is opposed to the horizontal time sense of the masses: "The temporality of authentic historicality . . . deprives the 'today' of its character as present, and weans one from the conventionalities of the 'they.' When, however, one's existence is inauthentically historical, it is loaded down with the legacy of a 'past' which has become unrecognizable, and it seeks the modern." For inauthentic historicality, in "awaiting the next thing . . . has already forgotten the old one. The 'they' evades choice."[76]

Even more interesting than these parallels to Bergson and Heidegger are the similarities between Hofmannsthal's concept of memory and that of Kierkegaard, similarities that make it very clear how Hofmannsthal could later "discover" Kierkegaard as both a source and an inspiration for *Der Schwierige*.[77] To begin with, although Kierkegaard was

[76] Martin Heidegger, *Being and Time*, trans. J. Macquarrie and E. Robinson (Oxford, 1967), pp. 435, 444. The inherent romanticism of Heidegger's quest for Being also leads him to some rather grandiose syntheses, ones whose abstract generality detracts from their existential impact. Heidegger's complex vision of authentic "historicality," for instance, appears to encompass Hofmannsthal's "past," the existentialist's "future-directed present," Nietzsche's monumental, antiquarian, and critical types of historiology (*Being and Time*, p. 448), and what Kierkegaard called "repetition."

[77] Hamburger, in his article on Hofmannsthal's library (pp. 37, 75), points out that although definite proof of Hofmannsthal's having read Kierkegaard before 1905 is lacking, it is still a possibility; for marked and annotated copies of *Stadien auf dem Lebensweg* (1886) and *Zur Psychologie der Sünde, der Bekehrung und des Glaubens* (1890; contains *The Concept of Dread* and the *Philosophical Fragments*) as well as a copy of the *Tagebuch des Verführers* (1903)

90

primarily a Protestant preacher and Hofmannsthal a Catholic poet, both men were essentially pitted against the same historical trends, namely the levelling of values, man's submergence in the anonymous collectivity of "the public," and the stripping of his temporal coordinates to those of the totally "secularized" present. Both responded to this with a general summons to an ethical, spiritual form of Bildung for the fast-disappearing individual, stressing in turn a strongly psychological view of time and memory. In *Either/ Or*, for example, Kierkegaard comments that "anxiety always involves a reflection upon time, for I cannot be anxious about the present, but only about the past or the future," a statement very similar to that made by Hofmannsthal in his essay "Furcht." (The parallel to Kierkegaard's concept of dread we have already pointed out.) Moreover, just as Hofmannsthal describes Electra's plight as the tragedy of one who cannot forget (PIII, 139), so Kierkegaard, in his reflections on Antigone, concludes that the "memory of her father is the cause of her death."[78] Furthermore, Hofmannsthal's notion of vertical time, with its voluntary, ethical form of recollection, would correspond to Kierkegaard's unique interpretation of religious repent-

---

were in his library. For the influence of Kierkegaard on *Der Schwierige* see Hamburger, pp. 71-75. For further information on the relationship of Hofmannsthal to Kierkegaard see Kobel, who mentions that by 1895 Hofmannsthal had read at least one part of the *Stadien*, that he asked Schnitzler in 1904 for a copy of *Entweder/Oder*, and that he quoted in his diary (A, 141) from the *Buch des Richters*, a selection from Kierkegaard's journals that appeared in 1905, translated by C. Schrempf. Kobel also points out (pp. 92-93, 123-124, 360) that Kierkegaard mentions "Präexistenz" in the *Philosophical Fragments* and the *Buch des Richters*. In general, however, the most striking elements in Hofmannsthal's relationship to Kierkegaard are parallels, not proven influences, as Kobel himself admits in his chapter on *Der Abenteurer und die Sängerin*.

[78] Sören Kierkegaard, *Either/Or*, I, 153, 162.

ance: that one might repent oneself (in the sense of remembering with contrition) "back into the family, back into the race, until he finds himself in God."[79]

By far the most interesting parallel to Hofmannsthal, however, lies in Kierkegaard's triadic conception of the spheres of existence, as put forth both in *Stages on Life's Way* (1845) and *Either/Or* (1843). In Kierkegaard's view there exist three basic modes of consciousness or ways of life: the aesthetic, the ethical, and the religious. Although these stages can also be understood as designating historical periods, the emphasis, as always in Kierkegaard, is largely on their relevance to the life of the individual. The first stage, that of the aesthetic way of life, he characterizes as the attitude that involves a childlike immediacy to the world, the capacity to live each passing moment to the full. Although Kierkegaard uses the examples of Don Juan and the Epicurean to illustrate this stage, we might just as easily substitute (as we have already implied in our second chapter) the aesthetic adventurers of Hofmannsthal's early plays: Claudio, Andrea, and the others whose devotion to the transitory present must constantly lead them to ethical betrayals. The end of this stage—which is never outgrown by some individuals—is signalled by the sudden realization that there is an endless sameness about such a type of existence; it is without growth, without Bildung. At this point there is, in Kierkegaard's words, a sudden collapse into "despair," a process exemplified in Hofmannsthal's early plays and, even more poignantly, in a small sketch appropriately entitled "Gerechtigkeit" (1893). In this, the youthful poet, sitting musing in his springtime garden, is unex-

[79] Kierkegaard, *Either/Or*, II, 220; it is interesting to note that we need only replace Kierkegaard's theological terms with the ontological categories of Heidegger to arrive at the idea that we must recall the truth of Being.

pectedly confronted by an angel; taken aback, he tries to defend his existence by referring to his exalted moments of aesthetic communion with the world; failing to do so, however, he is suddenly overcome by a crushing awareness of his tragic inadequacy (PI, 121).

The despair over the aesthetic stage of life brings about a conversion to the so-called ethical stage, keynoted for Kierkegaard by the awakening of memory.[80] The difference in the two attitudes—that between a preoccupation with the "I" and an awareness of the "Thou"—is roughly the same as that between *Verwandlung* and *Treue* as formulated by Hofmannsthal in his essay "Ariadne." Kierkegaard, admitting that there also exists a form of recollection in the aesthetic stage, points out that ethical recollection involves "effort and responsibility." His third and final stage, the religious, can only be entered upon with "fear and trembling," much as Abraham entered upon his faith in God when he was called upon to sacrifice his son Isaac. It is a mode of existence characterized above all by a seemingly irrational and highly subjective faith in an inner god; its manner of recollection assumes the religious form of repentance.[81] In Hofmannsthal, this stage, although perhaps not as immediately evident as the other two, is actually touched upon in the same essay. For when he explains how Ariadne could "forget" Theseus for Bacchus, he is virtually describing how the truth of the individual must always transcend the common morality, from which it is tragically separated by the "Delphic abyss" (PIII, 139-140). This point is exactly the same as that made by Kierkegaard when he speaks of the irrational "leap" from the ethical sphere to the religious. Thus Ariadne is for Hofmannsthal what Abra-

[80] *Ibid.*, 234.

[81] Sören Kierkegaard, *Stages on Life's Way*, trans. W. Lowrie (New York, 1967), pp. 28, 31.

ham was for Kierkegaard, and whereas Kierkegaard's personal solution for overcoming the existential gulf was to espouse the Christian faith, Hofmannsthal's, as we shall see, was to create what he called "mythological operas."

Hofmannsthal's well-known social comedy *Der Schwierige* (1921), on which Kierkegaard's influence is undisputed, provides an excellent summary of the parallels we have been talking about, in particular with regard to the role of memory. From Hofmannsthal's jottings in his own copy of the *Stages on Life's Way*, we know that he intended to portray in the figures of Hans Karl and Antoinette the difference, in Kierkegaard's terms, between true recollection and mere mechanical memory (*Erinnerung* and *Gedächtnis*).[82] Memory, for Kierkegaard, represents "immediacy and comes immediately to one's aid, whereas recollection comes only by reflection." Thus "memory makes life unconcerned. Unconcernedly, one passes through the most ludicrous metamorphoses."[83] Antoinette, in other words, with just such a "memory," is directly related to the youthful forgetters in Hofmannsthal's earlier works, those figures completely devoid of ethical or spiritual dimensions. "The moment," she says, quoting an earlier adventurer of Hofmannsthal's, "is everything" (LII, 249).[84] Hans Karl, on the other hand, as one who reflects and recollects, is caught in his relationship with Helene between the impossibility of forgetting her and his fearful hesitancy to remember her. This is clear from Hofmannsthal's reference to the passage in "Guilty?/Not Guilty?" where Kierkegaard writes: "Remembrance . . . is like a judgment on my head. . . . Did

[82] See Hamburger, "Hofmannsthals Bibliothek," p. 71. Kierkegaard's distinction between the two types of memory may in turn derive from Aristotle's short treatise, "On Memory and Reminiscence."

[83] Kierkegaard, *Stages*, pp. 30, 28.

[84] Cf. the Baron's words (DI, 451).

Adam dare to remind Eve, did he dare when he beheld thistles and thorns before his feet, did he dare to say to Eve, 'No! It was not like this in Eden. Ah, dost thou remember?' Did Adam dare? Still less do I." This is directly followed by the statement: "Forget her?—that is impossible."[85] It is easy to interpret these words as referring to Hans Karl's recollection of a paradisal vision that he had experienced when he was momentarily buried alive in the trenches during the war, and in which Helene had been revealed to him (in an epiphany-like moment of hypermnesia similar to that experienced by many of Hofmannsthal's earlier characters) as his eternal wife (LII, 263).

Hans Karl's and Antoinette's counterparts in the drama are Helene and the clown Furlani, each of whom adheres to his own sense of time with a singleness of purpose and a mastery that neither of the former two possesses. Helene, who, unlike Hans Karl, has remained faithful in her love for him for the past six years, is one who can never forget; "the moment," for her, "just doesn't exist" (LII, 261). As in so many other figural pairs in Hofmannsthal, her *Treue* is the necessary complement to Antoinette's *Verwandlung* (as in the cases of the Empress and the dyer's wife in the *Frau ohne Schatten*, Maria and Mariquita in *Andreas*, and the Egyptian and Trojan Helens in *Die ägyptische Helena*). Furlani, a descendant (on a higher level) of Harlequin in *Ariadne* and of other such protean actor figures in Hofmannsthal, represents Antoinette's ability to live in the present, but raised to the higher power of art. For he possesses the capability of adapting himself in every moment to the desires of others (LII, 221). He enjoys, as it were, Antoinette's unconcernedness and nonchalance, but in a way that requires twice as much art and effort (LII, 222).

Although much more could of course be said about the

[85] Kierkegaard, *Stages*, p. 322.

similarities between *Der Schwierige* and Kierkegaard (the figure of the young countess from the Heugasse who is forever *forgetting* the books rich in Bildung that she has read is a marvelous example, for instance, of both Kierkegaard's public and Hofmannsthal's new horizontal man [LII, 218]) this would lead us beyond our present concerns, and there still remains one more general, yet very important, parallel between the two writers that should be mentioned. It relates in particular to Hofmannsthal's concept of Bildung as he formulated it in his speech of 1927. We have already mentioned that Kierkegaard's final "solution" was a religious one, one which invoked the transcendent dimension of traditional Christianity. Hofmannsthal's own solution—that of a national, cultural Bildung—while not specifically religious, was equally transcendent in nature. It is a point made quite clearly in his speech: "All dualities into which the spirit has polarized life," he states, "must be overcome within the spirit and transformed into a spiritual unity; everything without us that has been divided must be brought into our own self and there recomposed into one" (PIV, 411-412). The conservative revolution that Hofmannsthal invokes, in other words, represents not only a "spiritualized politics," but a politics of religion as well. The "Bildung of a true nation" (PIV, 412) is posited on a national act of cultural "remembrance" that is truly religious in nature.

Not all of Hofmannsthal's postwar pleas for a recognition of the past assumed such an abstract, rhetorical form, however. On a more practical level, by directing his energies to a number of public undertakings, he was able to accomplish a great deal for the revival of culture buried in the collective memory. His primary method was to exploit as many media as were available for bringing art to the public—not in the Wagnerian sense of a *Gesamtkunstwerk*, but in the

Catholic baroque sense of a communal religious festival. Salzburg, where the *Festspiele* were initiated in 1920 with a production of Hofmannsthal's *Jedermann*, is only one of many examples. There were also the opera collaborations with Strauss, the literary journalism, the ballet collaborations, the social comedies, and even some attempts at film-making.[86] In general, of course, Hofmannsthal's move toward the theatrical—to gesture, action, music, stage-design, and dance—has been interpreted as an early symptom of the general intellectual "retreat from the word" in the twentieth century. While this is undoubtedly partly true, we must not overlook the obvious fact that a very real goal of Hofmannsthal's was simply to reach out and touch the indifferent public, to shake them loose from their moorings in the shallow waters of the present, and to refresh their cultural memory.

The last period in which Hofmannsthal seems to have believed in the possibility of a strictly literary Bildung, one without the aid of public performances, was the period before the war. This fact emerges most clearly from a book he published in 1912, an anthology of classical novellas he edited for the general public, under the title of *Deutsche Erzähler*. In the foreword to the collection he makes one of his last concrete statements on the necessity and possibility of Bildung for the individual. Beginning with a polemic against the horizontal time of an age that "only wants to know of itself and idolizes the shallow concept of the contemporary," Hofmannsthal explains that it is the *older* German writers whom he has collected here. He continues with a plea for an awakening of the vertical sense of time in the individual, and thus for an awareness of Bildung: "In the

---

[86] Namely, *Der Rosenkavalier* and *Das fremde Mädchen*, as well as a sketch for a film on Defoe. See also Hofmannsthal's interesting essay on the film as dream-medium, "Der Ersatz für die Träume" (PIV, 44 ff.).

single individual there is nothing purely present, development is everything. . . . The present is broad, the past deep; the breadth is disconcerting, whereas the depth delights; why should we always remain on the surface? When with dear friends, I want to explore their childhood, to hear what they were before I met them and knew them—not to ask after a thousand indifferent people whom they met today" (PIII, 109-110). Yet the words, as Hofmannsthal himself may have sensed at the time, already have a slightly hollow ring to them, an undertone of apprehension that true Bildung may be a thing of the past. For at two crucial points in the foreword he shifts his appeal to the collective abstraction of the *Volk*, a tacit admission that Bildung in the private sphere is already endangered. Furthermore, in the same year, 1912, he also took up *Andreas* once more, wrote a major part of it, and then apparently put it aside, never to complete its final sections. Very shortly, the "dark years at hand" that Hofmannsthal prophesies in the essay became a European reality.

PART II *Andreas*

Six The Novel and the Two Hofmannsthals

The whole man must move at once.

*M*UCH LIKE Schiller, who produced only one novel, and that a surrealistic fragment set in Venice, Hofmannsthal has left us with only *Andreas oder die Vereinigten.* Considering the fact that he had published his first poems when he was sixteen and still in the *Gymnasium,* Hofmannsthal began the novel fairly late, for he was thirty-three when he first conceived of the idea, and approaching forty when he did the major work on it. The year of its conception (1907) was an extraordinarily productive one for him, for during it he wrote the important and thematically related essays "Erinnerung schöner Tage," "Die Wege und die Begegnungen," "Die Briefe des Zurückgekehrten," and "Furcht," and also began his first comedy, *Cristinas Heimreise*—which, like the novel, takes Venice as its setting. The previous December he had undertaken his lecture tour in Germany with "Der Dichter und diese Zeit," and in the following year he was to go to Greece and begin writing the "Augenblicke in Griechenland."

In late June of 1907, while at the Lido in Venice, Hofmannsthal made a start on the novel with a short, three-page draft entitled "Venezianisches Reisetagebuch des Herrn von N. (1779)," the only section of the novel written in first-person form. Inspiration for the work at the time, besides the stay in Venice itself, was his reading of two works: Philippe Monnier's *Venise au dix-huitième*

101

Siècle (Paris, 1907) and Morton Prince's *The Dissociation of a Personality* (New York, 1906). The major part of the novel, however, had to wait until 1912 and 1913 to be written. In these years, which also saw his increasing activity as a librettist for Strauss, Hofmannsthal apparently wrote "Die Dame mit dem Hündchen" and "Das venezianische Erlebnis des Herrn von N." (both about twenty-five pages long), as well as the main part of the novel, *Andreas oder die Vereinigten*, a section approximately eighty pages in length subtitled "Die wunderbare Freundin." Although some of the notes may well have been written in later years, specific dates still remain a matter of conjecture. In general, much of the novel's genesis is shrouded in uncertainty and must remain so until the eventual publication of the *Nachlass*.[1] As it stands, we can only surmise that the completed work would not have exceeded perhaps three or four times the length of the section we possess.

The fragment was first published in the periodical *Corona* in 1930, a year after the poet's death, and two years later it appeared in book form in Berlin, with a perceptive epilogue by Jakob Wasserman, Hofmannsthal's friend and fellow-writer. Yet the book was doomed to further obscurity, for with the rise of the National Socialists, for whom Wasserman and Hofmannsthal were both Jewish and

---

[1] For accounts of the genesis—as much as we know of it—see Richard Alewyn, *Über Hugo von Hofmannsthal* (Göttingen, 1963), pp. 126-127; Werner Volke, *Hugo von Hofmannsthal* (Hamburg, 1967), p. 113; Karl Gautschi, *Hugo von Hofmannsthals Romanfragment 'Andreas'* (diss. Zürich, 1965), pp. 8-9; Helmut A. Fiechtner, ed., *Hugo von Hofmannsthal: Der Dichter im Spiegel der Freunde* (Bern, 1963), p. 31. Not the least of the difficulties involved in determining the exact dates of the work is the unreliability of Hofmannsthal's own memory; in a 1917 letter to Rudolf Pannwitz, for instance, he speaks of the novel as being set in the year of Maria Theresa's death (1780) and as having a twenty-three-year-old hero (Andreas is actually twenty-two and the story takes place in 1778).

decadent, the novel was to remain out of sight until after the war, when Herbert Steiner republished it along with many of Hofmannsthal's other works. Despite these vicissitudes in its existence (both before and after Hofmannsthal's death) and despite its brief compass of eighty pages, the fragment has drawn constant praise from writers as well as critics. Wasserman compares it to Novalis' *Heinrich von Ofterdingen* and to Büchner's *Lenz*; Stefan Zweig refers to it as the "torso of possibly the most beautiful novel in the German language"; Richard Alewyn describes it as "eighty pages of the most vibrant prose that has ever been written in the German language"; and other critics have spoken of it as "the most beautiful example of German prose in our time," as the "most tantalizingly enthralling of his many unfinished works," and as a piece that "alone would be sufficient to ensure him a place among the greatest German writers."[2]

Quite apart from its richly imagistic and rhythmic prose, however, *Andreas* is important because of its central position in Hofmannsthal's overall development, in particular with regard to the "aesthetic" versus the "ethical" poet. Criticism, for many years, viewed Hofmannsthal as an aesthetic prodigy of *fin de siècle* Vienna. He was, in the eyes of more than one critic, a "combination of Edwardian Werther and Viennese Dorian Gray";[3] his poems, furthermore, celebrated beauty "as the last religion of an age that foresees its own downfall and seeks refuge in the arts." His

[2] Jakob Wasserman, "Nachwort" to *Andreas* (Berlin, 1932), p. 177; Stefan Zweig, *Die Welt von Gestern* (Berlin, 1962), p. 57; Richard Alewyn, "Nachwort" to *Andreas* (Frankfurt a. M., 1961), p. 139; Edgar Hederer, *Hugo von Hofmannsthal* (Frankfurt a. M., 1960), p. 19; Michael Hamburger, "Introduction" to the *Poems and Verse Plays* of Hofmannsthal (New York, 1961), p. xix; Volke, p. 115.

[3] Barbara W. Tuchman, *The Proud Tower* (New York, 1966), p. 325.

works belonged to an age in which the "glorious opalescence of things hangs, as in an impressionistic painting, like a thin veil before the void."[4]

Such statements would naturally call forth a reaction, and there were also those critics who proposed to see the ethical Hofmannsthal, the Hofmannsthal concerned less with word-magic than with the everyday magic of marriage, love, and children as well as with the moral problems of the aesthetic existence. Yet whereas the former critics had succumbed to the myopic view that the moralism of this gentle cultivator of an autumnal civilization had been but an "extraneous . . . resolution,"[5] those in the latter group often tended toward overemphasis of the simplistic schemes of *Ad me ipsum*. Supporting their arguments by these notes, they stressed the insight that one must eventually pass from the dreamy limbos of youth into the harsh realities of manhood, a process that according to Hofmannsthal is to be accomplished either via the introverted mysticism of a Chandos or along the extroverted path of social action, dramatic writing, and/or marriage (as in the case of Hofmannsthal himself). Such critics emphasized "existence" only, rather than its dialectical connection with "pre-existence"; instead of focussing on the creative anguish of a poet inhabiting the difficult ground between the temple of art and that of life, they spoke of his successful exit from the darkness of the temple into the bustle and light of the street outside.[6] Neither Hofmannsthal's general views on Bildung

[4] Walter Muschg, *Von Trakl zu Brecht* (Munich, 1961), p. 95.

[5] Erich Heller, *Thomas Mann: The Ironic German* (Cleveland, 1961), p. 26.

[6] See "Hofmannsthals Wandlung" (1949) and also "Der Tod des Ästheten" (1944) in Alewyn's *Über Hugo von Hofmannsthal*. Despite their somewhat schematized view, these essays provide an excellent appraisal of the younger Hofmannsthal. It should be emphasized, however, that Alewyn was not the first to recognize Hof-

nor his own personal development gains greatly in significance or interest by citing the two-step process (youth to maturity) described in *Ad me ipsum.*

The very complexity of Hofmannsthal's works, in other words, has often been ignored by critics who have felt themselves compelled to side with either the moralists or the aesthetes. Thus pious eulogies to Hofmannsthal as a second Goethe have alternated with glorifications of his cult of Viennese aestheticism, just as attacks on the writer have shifted from moralistic indignation at his portraits of Nietzschean vitalism (*Elektra*) to existential protest at his revival of medieval Christianity (*Jedermann*). Through such reductive tactics, however, critics not only turn complexity into mere polemic but inevitably reveal more of themselves than they do of Hofmannsthal's works. In view of the protean spread of Hofmannsthal's development, undoubtedly one of the most sane and fruitful approaches is that suggested by Michael Hamburger. Seeing in Hofmannsthal "one of the most complex and enigmatic minds of the half-century," and in his works a veritable *Weltliteratur* in the Goethean sense, Hamburger advances a plea for single interpretations: "every new reading of any one of his works in the light of another reveals new interrelations, new intricacies of texture and allusion, new seeming contradictions and paradoxes."[7]

Andreas, perhaps more than any other single work of Hofmannsthal's, is deeply representative of the breadth of interest and sensibility Hamburger refers to. Aside from its

---

mannsthal's "moral" qualities, for Rudolf Borchardt as well as Rudolf Alexander Schröder had indicated the same in their essays of some years earlier. See, for example, Borchardt's "Rede über Hofmannsthal" (1902), and Schröder's "In memoriam Hugo von Hofmannsthal" (1929).

[7] Hamburger, "Introduction" to the *Poems and Verse Plays,* p. lxiii.

innate artistic qualities, it is a product of the Hofmannsthal who was neither "early" nor "late," neither carefree aesthete nor tragic moralist. Extending over the vital middle period, the period that has been least explored by critics so far, the novel helps us to relate his most diverse ideas to a single center, particularly in the light of his own conviction of the "extraordinary unity" of his works (A, 237). A consideration of the novel allows us to discuss his chief themes— those of memory and Bildung—without resorting expressly to a dichotomy of artist and moralist or to any of the "cheap antitheses such as 'art' and 'life,' aesthete and non-aesthete" (A, 139), as Hofmannsthal himself puts it. Not only does *Andreas* represent the fruition of certain earlier ethical ideas, such as that of the recollected self and the allomatic quality of love, but it also contains the beginnings of a conscious attempt to articulate a religious or spiritual dimension in experience. More than any other of his works, *Andreas* invites Hofmannsthal's own critical approach, which would view "works of art as the continual emanation of a personality . . . as *heures*, rays of light that a soul casts upon the world" (A, 139).

Like so many other German novels before it, *Andreas* is based on the structural principle of the *Bildungsreise*, the sentimental and cultural journey commencing in youthful wanderlust and culminating in marriage and maturity. The young hero, the twenty-two-year-old Andreas von Ferschengelder, who has been living with his upper-class parents in Vienna, is being sent to Italy one September on just such a journey to complete his education. The year is 1778, a period of Austrian history much-favored in Hofmannsthal's works. Empress Maria Theresa is on the throne, Mozart has just succeeded Gluck as court composer in Vienna, and Venice, Andreas' destination, is not yet part of Italy, but an independent city-state lying at the gateway to the mysterious Orient—rich in the splendors of the Byzantine as well as of the Renaissance. Andreas is no further on his journey than the village of Villach in the Carinthian Alps of southern Austria when he is suddenly confronted by an offensive and unsavory servant by the ironic name of Gotthilff, a surly twenty-five-year-old who half forces, half flatters Andreas into buying a horse for him and hiring him as an escort to Venice. On the first afternoon of their journey, however, Gotthilff's horse is injured in a stumble and on the following morning the two of them are forced to seek lodging at a stately farmstead located in an Alpine valley, an estate owned by the Finazzer family. That afternoon Andreas becomes acquainted with Romana, the seventeen-year-old daughter of the family, and immediately develops a deep love for her. Late that night, the entire household is rudely awakened by the screams of one of the maids—the one, in fact, to whom Gotthilff had attached himself immediately after their arrival. The family and Andreas arrive at a scene of horror, for the maid's room is filled with the smoke from a burning bed to which the maid, half-naked, has been tied. From her hysterical words they learn that Gotthilff, after first poisoning the Finazzers' dog to silence him, had attacked her, and then had made off with Andreas' horse as well as a large part of the travel money given to Andreas by his parents, which Andreas had sewn into the saddlebag. Moreover, the lame horse left by Gotthilff in the stables turns out to be one that had been stolen from the Finazzers a short time before.

Andreas, overcome with shame and remorse at these events and now without a horse, is forced to remain yet another day and a half at the farmstead until he can obtain a ride with a wagon passing through the valley. During this time he sees Romana only once more—when they briefly kiss goodbye in the stables on the last afternoon, Romana

107

barefoot, silent, and struggling to hold back her tears. Shortly afterward, on his way down the valley, Andreas experiences a sudden mystical vision of his love for the girl whom he has now known for only three days, a vision in which he sees Romana as a "living being, a center, and around her . . . a paradise no less real than the opposite side of the valley which towered above." Moreover, he spies an eagle circling in the last rays of the setting sun high over the darkening valley, and (in an oblique reference to the title of the novel) he senses "that seen from high enough all those who are separated are united, and that loneliness is only an illusion" (E, 162).

On September 17th, early in the morning, Andreas arrives in Venice, and immediately takes a room with a noble but impoverished family (reminiscent of the family portrayed in Hofmannsthal's "Brief des letzten Contarin"). Both Count Gasparo Prampero and his wife have menial jobs in the theater of St. Samuel directly across the canal, whereas Nina, their blonde twenty-one-year-old daughter who was formerly an actress, now supports herself comfortably as a high-class prostitute in an apartment elsewhere in the city. Andreas is given her former room, where the scene-painter and stage designer Zorzi has been staying temporarily. The younger daughter, the fifteen-year-old Zustina, as Andreas is shocked to discover, is offering her virginity as first prize in a grand lottery at the coming Mardi Gras in order to help out the family financially; he is even more taken aback when she apologizes to him that she isn't able to offer him a ticket.

The remainder of the novel relates the various encounters Andreas has on his first day in the city. He spends the morning lounging in his room and recalling his three-day stay in the Alps with the Finazzers, and during the afternoon he goes out with the painter Zorzi to visit Nina. On his way to her apartment he accidentally makes two strange acquaintances. In a small coffee-house he first meets Sacramozo, a forty-year-old Maltese Knight clad in the black robes (without the white cross) of the Order of the Knights Hospitalers and rumored to be allied with both the Jesuits and the Freemasons. Not only is Sacramozo's brother the person who is in charge of the lottery for Zustina's virginity, but Sacramozo himself, as we know from the notes, is to be Andreas' spiritual mentor during his sojourn in Venice. Somewhat later that afternoon, in a small, empty church in an out-of-the-way square, Andreas catches sight of a woman who he later learns is Maria. She is the young attractive, dark-haired widow (the "lady with the little dog" referred to in the title of one of the drafts) with whom Sacramozo corresponds and who, at the very moment that Andreas sees her in the church, is undergoing a nervous breakdown, falling into severe schizophrenia. On his way to Nina's, Andreas encounters Maria once again, yet this time in what appears to be a dream-vision, for he suddenly catches sight of her overhead, through the trellis in a tiny courtyard. The ensuing visit with Nina, except for a few dream-like, compulsive recollections of Gotthilff and Romana, is entirely uneventful, and the novel breaks off with Andreas alone once more in the empty, narrow streets of Venice, filled with the strange desire to search for the young Maria, the "wonderful mistress" (*wunderbare Freundin*) alluded to in the subtitle of the novel.

In terms of plot, then, *Andreas* appears to be just one more historical novel of picaresque adventures set in foreign lands. Yet what a plot summary conceals are the work's two most singular aspects: its extraordinarily modern, spatial structure and its highly symbolic mode of narration. Fully half of the eighty completed pages of the fragment deal, in the form of a flashback, with Andreas' adventures in the Alps; the episodes with Romana and Gotthilff, in other words, are given to us through the internal focus of

Andreas' memory, as he sits musing for an hour or so in his room in Venice. In the Venetian scenes, on the other hand, style and narrative standpoint strike the reader as disturbingly modern and surrealistic, for the technique employed is very similar to that of both E.T.A. Hoffmann and Kafka, and the themes involved are those of reality-confusion, projected psychological disturbances, and split personality; the figure of Maria, for example, is actually Maria-Mariquita, an Eve White *and* an Eve Black. Through its symbolic form and style, the action throughout the novel is thus effectively shifted from the outer landscape of epic narrative (as exemplified in earlier Bildungsromane such as *Wilhelm Meister*, for instance) to the complex inscape of twentieth-century fiction, with its more psychological, more "confessional" Bildung. Andreas' development does not press ever outward toward a Goethean fulfillment of the total personality, but rather inward, through the re-assemblage of certain critical moments in the past, to an ultimate renewal and reassertion of the self.

In sum, the fascination of *Andreas* lies in the fact that it represents a sort of literary crossroads of the two traditions of the epic quest and the confession. On the one hand, there are endless thematic parallels to earlier novels belonging more to the adventure pattern: Sacramozo as a latter-day masonic emissary of the *Bundesroman* variety; Maria and Mariquita (the spiritual and the sensual) as a reflection of Keller's Anna and Judith or of Goethe's Beautiful Soul and Philine; or the entire fragment as a modern version of Schiller's *Geisterseher*, which also incorporates a Venetian setting, masked figures and secret intrigues, vanishing ladies in churches, perplexing interactions between the real and the imaginary, philosophical discussions of Bildung, and a Sacramozo-like figure called the Armenian. (Hofmannsthal had, interestingly enough, included this work in his anthology of 1912.) On the other hand, however, with its highly self-conscious protagonist, its stress on compulsive recollection and feelings of guilt, and its vacillation between epic narration and first-person memoir (in the first draft), the novel approaches more modern forms of the Bildungs-roman such as Rilke's *Malte*.

In terms of Hofmannsthal's own personality, as we have already indicated, the fragment centers on the creative mid-dle period of his life, that time when his ideas on the ethical dimensions of memory were developing and being ex-pressed in the essays. Furthermore, particularly in its form, the fragment mirrors precisely the tension that Broch saw at work in so many of Hofmannsthal's writings, namely, the tension between the poet's great capacity for self-suppres-sion (a gift similar to Keats's Negative Capability, but which Broch views as more of an *incapability*) and his deep inner need for self-confession.[8] The novel, which begins as a visual, epic story, ends as an open notebook, more mirror of the writer-narrator himself than of the fictional protago-nist. In the very fact of its incompletion it reflects Hof-mannsthal's undeniable distance from the classic Goethean pattern of the Bildungsroman; as he himself was to admit less than a year after he had begun *Andreas*, anyone who wants to appreciate *Wilhelm Meister* must "leave behind much of himself, of the atmosphere of his [present] life"; above all, he must "call to mind his 'transfigured self' . . . , his eternal, unconditional humanity."[9] Yet in spite of all this,

[8] See Hermann Broch's "Introduction" to Hofmannsthal's *Selected Prose*, trans. M. Hottinger and T. & J. Stern (New York, 1952). Broch, whose distinction is between (visual) "I-suppression" and (musical) "I-confession," sees Hofmannsthal as arriving at a con-fessional poetry only in the essays and in *Der Turm*.

[9] (PII, 330); see also the *Zurückgekehrter*'s comment on such novels as *Wilhelm Meister*: "Was in diesen Romanen abgespiegelt war, erschien mir immer wie im Spiegelbild, unendlich vertieft, verklärt, beruhigt" (PII, 279).

for most readers it is probably true that, "in the difficult and confused moments of their lives, Goethe will fail them" (PII, 328).

In the spring of 1907, before Hofmannsthal left for Venice and his first work on *Andreas*, he heard Rilke give a reading in a Viennese bookshop from *Malte*, his current work in progress, and in November of the same year Rilke visited Hofmannsthal at his home in Rodaun. Whether or not Hofmannsthal was actually influenced by Rilke in his plans for a novel is impossible to determine, but in any case his own work was actually to bear far more similarity to Rilke's than to Goethe's.[10] In fact, Hofmannsthal's as well as Rilke's distance from Goethe might best be described by paraphrasing Hofmannsthal's own comment on Shakespeare's distance from Dante: whereas the older poet's figures "are placed in a gigantic architectonic system," those of the more modern writer "are oriented not to the stars but to themselves; and they carry within themselves hell, purgatory, and heaven" (PII, 148). It is precisely this inner world of the personality, in particular as it is depicted in Hofmannsthal's own protagonist Andreas, that we will investigate in the following chapter.

[10] In this connection it is interesting to note that the Danish writer Jens Peter Jacobsen (1847-1885), who exercised such a profound influence on Rilke, was also known to Hofmannsthal, who was particularly impressed by the deep psychological insights in Jacobsen's novels (A, 100).

Seven

Andreas as Hero: The Dissociated Self
and the Unresolved Past

Andreas, like most protagonists of the Bildungsroman, bears a strong family resemblance to his
creator. Like Hofmannsthal, he is the only child of a
Viennese family; he is a member of the lesser nobility
(for his grandfather, like Hofmannsthal's great-grand-
father, had been ennobled); his psychological difficulties
and uncertainties reflect very closely Hofmannsthal's
own problems at approximately the same age, in particular with regard to his ultimate choice of career; and the
peasant girl Romana Finazzer may well be modeled in
part on the Romana whom Hofmannsthal met in August
of 1896 while on vacation at Aussee in the Austrian Alps
when he, like Andreas, was twenty-two years old (see
PIII, 169). On the other hand, Andreas possesses literary
forebears as well, the most important of whom is undoubtedly Wilhelm Meister. Not only is the novel set in
the same period, the late eighteenth century, but Andreas, who is the same age as Wilhelm and is interested
in the theater, has also embarked on a journey toward
education in its broadest sense.

Yet we might pause at this point and ask ourselves if
such literary parallels really tell us much about the novel
as it stands. "An Austrian *Wilhelm Meister*"—such is the
way Jakob Wasserman describes the novel in his epilogue to its first edition, and countless other critics, undoubtedly in an attempt to assert the high literary qual-

ity of the fragment, have followed suit. Karl Gautschi, for instance, writes that Andreas is the "ideal hero of a Bildungsroman, for the narrative significantly begins at that point where the young man is setting out into the world to begin his apprenticeship."[11] Yet we must question if such analogies afford us any real insight into the novel. The Bildungsroman, like any genre, is not a fixed form, and it is often the departures from a tradition that are more instructive for an understanding of the individual work than are the parallels. Andreas' character, for example, is perhaps best understood if we contrast it to Wilhelm Meister's.

As we have already suggested at the beginning of this study, Wilhelm's process of Bildung is largely one of unconscious growth. As "nature's darling" he basically enjoys a whole and lively self from the very beginning: "From youth onward," he asserts, "my subconscious wish has been the cultivation of my individual self, *just as I am*" (italics mine).[12] In Andreas' case, however, the situation is vastly and tragically different. "Andreas' two halves, which are split asunder" is the note that begins one draft of the novel (E, 195); and again, "One thing in particular he found difficult: to arrive at himself, and his whole being was occupied with this task" (E, 226). Andreas' ultimate goal, in other words, is Wilhelm's starting point, the ability to state unequivocally "ganz wie ich da bin." This radical difference between the two heroes is also implicit in a note by Hofmannsthal in his journal, in which he describes Goethe's Bildungsroman as follows: "Two great epochs: one of wandering, one with direction. . . . The former has an element of childlike comedy; indiscriminate use of the words 'happiness', 'I', 'people'. . . . My transition, Edgar [Karg von Beben-

[11] Gautschi, p. 15.

[12] J. W. Goethe, *Werke*, ed. Erich Trunz (Hamburg, 1965), VII, 77, 290.

burg], military service, new choice of career" (A, 127). What Hofmannsthal here designates as the naive first part of Goethe's novel is precisely what is missing from his own. Andreas, whose situation is far from being characterized by such easy words as *Glück*, *Ich*, and *Menschen*, suffers intensely from "traces of anhedonia, loss of a sense of values, confusion of ideas" (E, 221), from a "strange lack of self-confidence" (E, 199), and from a "growing aversion to people" (E, 197). In short, Goethe's holistic concept of organic growth implied in Wilhelm Meister's development is radically absent from that of Andreas; the bright scenes of the entelechial journey to selfhood have been replaced by the pathology of a split personality.

Furthermore, in ironic counterpoint to *Wilhelm Meister*, in which Wilhelm's cultural wanderings are undertaken expressly *against* the wishes of his merchant-minded father, Andreas' journey to Venice is precisely "due to the calculating snobbishness of his father" (E, 195). He has been launched upon the quest for culture merely for the sake of social propriety: "And now they had sent him abroad on a costly journey—for what purpose?—to meet foreign peoples, to observe strange customs, to polish his manners. But all of these things were only means to an end" (E, 144-145). Moreover, even Andreas' relationship to the theater bears little resemblance to Wilhelm's: instead of harboring dreams of founding a National Theater Company, he simply desires to "live near a theater" (E, 195).

Hopelessly distant from that wholeness of being that characterizes Wilhelm, Andreas suffers from a psychological split that Hofmannsthal himself had undoubtedly experienced as well. On the one hand Andreas is at the mercy of moments in which he is consumed by an overwhelming self-consciousness, moments usually signalled by an extremely hesitant and uncertain manner: "Immediately

115

it seemed superfluous to have mentioned this; he was over-come with embarrassment and his Italian became confused" (E, 114); and again: "But once more Andreas said one word too many, because he felt he had reacted too rudely . . . but the last sentence was already too much . . . and took its revenge" (E, 124-125). Even his questions are fragmen-tary: "Which one?" (E, 119); "So you're gentry, and the coat of arms . . . is yours?" (E, 134); "What kind of man is that?" (E, 149). On the other hand, particularly when he is together with Romana, Andreas appears totally devoid of self-consciousness, to the point where it seems that he is being led about by the hand like a puppet: "She took An-dreas by the hand" (E, 135); "Until Romana . . . pulled Andreas along by the hand" (E, 136); "She drew him there and told him to sit down next to her" (E, 137); "She . . . drew him gently to her. . . . She let him go and then pulled him softly to her again" (E, 139).

This unhappy split in Andreas' character between anx-ious self-consciousness and total passivity is merely part of a larger pattern of schizophrenic tendencies. "On the one hand," as the notes tell us, he is "attracted to the sensual, on the other to the ideal" (E, 222). His labile personality—"an insignificant framework, a scarecrow" (E, 228)—is sus-pended between those tragic polarities of time that so obsessed Hofmannsthal. "To Andreas time is everything," Hofmannsthal notes,[13] and with these words strikes to the heart of Andreas' problems and anxieties. For unlike the dancers, actors, and adventurers of the early works, An-dreas is supremely conscious of time, particularly of the time of his own childhood. Like the *Zurückgekehrter*, whose letters were written in the same year that the novel was begun, Andreas is painfully aware of how "strange and

[13] Theodor Wieser, "Der Malteser in Hofmannsthals 'Andreas'," *Euphorion*, 51 (1957), 407.

deep everything is that happens to us in childhood"
(PII, 295). Indeed, he possesses powers of recollection
bordering on those of the poet; as he states at the very beginning of the first version of the novel, "I remember things
very exactly—always had a good memory, won the Grand
Cross of Excellence at school because I could recite all my
mother's maids, and all my grandfather's minerals, and the
names of the stars in Orion" (E, 192). Like the *Zurückgekehrter*, he also discovers within himself memories of
ancestors, and yet these only serve to remind him of his own
unresolved self, for together with the recollection of his
revered and heroic grandfather Andreas there returns the
image of his cruel, self-seeking Uncle Leopold as well. His
memories of the Finazzerhof are similarly filled with horror
as well as happiness, for although the flashback concludes
with a transfigured vision of Romana, it commences with
the frightening aspect of Gotthilff's evil face. Moreover,
these memories of the Finazzerhof provide the Venetian
episodes with a form of symbolic background. On the first
afternoon in Venice, for instance, when Andreas is visiting
Nina in her apartment, he suddenly, involuntarily, recalls
Romana: "The farm girl Romana appeared before him, only
to vanish immediately again into thin air" (E, 187), and a
few moments later he is confronted by the equally unpre-
meditated vision of Gotthilff: "The face of the servant
Gotthilff appeared, grinning at him; the beautiful moment
had vanished" (E, 190).

These unresolved, discordant memories that form the
backdrop for Andreas' Venetian experiences are also reflected in the configuration of character-types he meets
there; basically, they represent the temporal tensions inherent within himself. The split personality of Maria-Mariquita, for instance, embodies the crucial dialectic of remembering and forgetting. Maria possesses an extremely

117

powerful memory, involuntarily recalling even unpleasant experiences. Not only does this sensitivity of hers to the past touch upon the poetic—like the poet of "Manche freilich," she cannot escape even the "silent fall of distant stars" (E, 206)—but it also borders on the tragic, for the notes hint at an Electra-like fate for her: "the possibility of dying a martyr's death, or of stagnation" (E, 206). On the other hand, when Maria occasionally senses the "Mariquita" within her she is overcome by a strange feeling of "living one's life to the full" (E, 245), much like the adventurer-type described in "Ariadne." For Mariquita, like Chrysothemis, represents "total forgetfulness" (E, 209). Like the dancer Zerbinetta, the earlier Faustian adventurers, and Antoinette in *Der Schwierige*, she "believes in the moment, and nothing else" (E, 208); "even her thoughts are pure pantomime" (E, 207). Maria and Mariquita, then, reflect the "antinomy of being and becoming" that Hofmannsthal perceived in Electra and Chrysothemis and that embodied for him the fundamental "incomprehensibility of time" (A, 217). As he comments in the notes to the novel, "It is again the basic problem of *Gestern*: fidelity, steadfastness, and change" (E, 207). Maria and her alter ego Mariquita exist at opposite sides of the Delphic abyss of existence.

The third major figure whom Andreas encounters in Venice, Sacramozo, reflects yet a third relationship to time, one perhaps best described as a highly spiritualized variety of the vertical time that plays so vital a role in Andreas' own Bildung. Not only does Sacramozo believe in a "*fluidum* of kinship" (E, 199), but he also experiences historical time as spatial and cumulative. "He knows that the body forgets nothing (likewise the macrocosm, the great body)" (E, 215), and he flatly rejects a cyclical view of time, displaying an "attentiveness to and reverence for things that do not return" (E, 218). Because no moment is ever totally lost, all experiences in the past are potentially present for him (E, 228), and thus a single occurrence can affect an entire lifetime (E, 223). Like the poet, he can appreciate "that which occurs only once" (E, 245); "everything serves him, even a landscape seen only once, a pool of dark water in the West Indies" (E, 215). As he instructs Andreas, "To be master of one's self means to have everything present, even the subliminal" (E, 245). Andreas' path to self-realization, however, is not to be identical with that of Sacramozo, but only analogous to it. "The antinomy of being and having," as Hofmannsthal points out, exists for Sacramozo "in the spiritual realm . . . just as it exists for Andreas in the human sphere" (E, 246). Sacramozo's conception of time and self is ultimately too Platonic to be equated with Hofmannsthal's own idea of Bildung, although the increasing emphasis on the figure of Sacramozo in the notes does reflect Hofmannsthal's own increasingly abstract, spiritual views on time and memory in later years. For Sacramozo perceives everywhere "the veiled image of Sais" (E, 245),[14] is possessed by a "burning desire for the purity of all things" (E, 245), and "moves within a time that is not fully present, and in a place not fully here" (E, 234); the act of perception, for him, in true Platonic fashion, is nothing but a re-cognition, a "recollection" (E, 202).

Despite the fact that his spiritual path thus diverges from that of Andreas, Sacramozo is to be of considerable help to his pupil in his quest for Bildung. He counsels Andreas, for instance, that "only he has a horror of the past, who, remaining at a lower level, imagines that it might all have

---

[14] Sais, an ancient capital of Lower Egypt and the center of various ancient mystery cults, is a common symbol in German literature, deriving largely from the eighteenth-century interest in the masonic and the occult. Cf. the motif of the "veil of truth" in Schiller's "Das verschleierte Bild zu Sais" and Novalis' "Die Lehrlinge zu Sais."

turned out otherwise" (E, 243). He also refers to "Andreas' reluctance . . . to recall his experiences with Gotthilff" (E, 243), and tries to bring to his attention "the soul's aversion to what it has recently experienced" (E, 202). Andreas must come to feel at every moment of his life, as Sacramozo does at the end of his, "that nothing he has done in his life has been in vain" (E, 219), he must learn to affirm "from one's present standpoint, the chain of experiences as necessary" (E, 244). For at present he "does not really believe in his experiences" (E, 222); "everything only *recalls* relationships, none really exist" (E, 247; my italics). Only when he succeeds in resolving and affirming *all* past experiences, including those with Gotthilff, will he attain that state Sacramozo terms "egocentricity at a higher stage" (E, 244). To arrive there, however, Andreas must first recognize a necessary and symbolic shape in his recollected experiences. His ultimate fate, as expressed in the final words of the notes, turns on the question of whether or not "these fragments in the kaleidoscope [of memory] can form a new pattern" (E, 247).[15]

[15] This striking metaphor for memory is also used by Henri Bergson, who compares the perceptual process in general to the ever-changing patterns in a kaleidoscope: "Our activity goes from an arrangement to a rearrangement, each time no doubt giving the kaleidoscope a new shake, but not interesting itself in the shake, and seeing only the new picture." *Creative Evolution*, trans. A. Mitchell (New York, Modern Library), p. 333.

EIGHT The Flashback: The Alps

Gotthilff and the Finazzers: The Dialectics of Experience (The First Day)

HE LONG flashback in *Andreas*, which forms roughly half the entire fragment, deserves extended treatment for several reasons. It is the only structurally complete section of the novel that we have, and its location near the very beginning of the work is obviously a strategic one with respect to the final shape of the narrative. Moreover, it also contains, thematically, the seeds of Andreas' entire future Bildung, for he cannot come to terms with either the present or the future until he has settled in his own mind exactly what happened and what role he played during his stay at the Finazzerhof, and until this is decided, he cannot come to terms with his problematic love for Romana. And finally, there is the fact that this section has largely been neglected by critics. Indeed, all three of the most important studies of *Andreas* concentrate almost exclusively on the Venetian episodes rather than on those involving Romana: Alewyn devotes his energies to the events in Venice, obviously because of his discovery of a source for the strange figure of Maria-Mariquita; Martini also chooses to focus his *explication de texte* upon paragraphs taken from the Venetian adventures; Gautschi, with the most comprehensive treatment, still devotes all but one of his six chapters to the figures whom Andreas meets in Venice.[16]

[16] Gautschi, *Hugo von Hofmannsthals Romanfragment 'Andreas'*; Alewyn, *Über Hugo von Hofmannsthal*; and Fritz Martini, *Das Wagnis der Sprache* (Stuttgart, 1954), pp. 225-257.

121

The obvious danger in emphasizing solely the Venetian section of the novel, however, is that it is all too easy to succumb to the fascinating challenge of correlating the jumble of appended notes and of reconstructing and projecting the imaginary end of the novel (something about which even Hofmannsthal himself was very likely uncertain). As it now stands, however, there is still a great deal we can say about Andreas' long and detailed recollection.

The Alpine events, which are far from being settled in the kaleidoscope of Andreas' memory, recur with compulsive and oppressive regularity—indeed, at least once a day after he has left the Finazzerhof. In fact, as soon as he is settled in his room in Venice on the very morning of his arrival, he finds himself recalling the journey. "He was ashamed of himself and shrank from the memory of the three disastrous days in Carinthia, but the face of the villainous servant already stood before him, and whether he wanted to or not, he was compelled to recall everything in minute detail from the very beginning: and so it happened, once a day, morning or evening" (E, 122). The long recollection itself is divided in the text into three sections: (1) the ride of a day and a half with the servant Gotthilff, (2) the afternoon with Romana and the night of the catastrophe, and (3) the following day and a half before his departure. Inwardly and thematically, however, it falls into three different sections corresponding to the "three disastrous days" of his visit, with the encounter with Gotthilff serving as a prelude or introduction. Indeed, the curve of the three days' events displays a dramatic symmetry. During the first day and night Andreas becomes involved in a dreadful series of events revolving about Gotthilff and Romana that culminates in the brutal scene of the fire in the maid's room; on the second, he wanders alone to the nearby village, overcome with despair and remorse at the previous day's events; and on the third day, following a prophetic and deeply symbolic dream in the early morning, he leaves for Venice, experiencing a sublime vision of Romana as he departs from the Finazzerhof.

Andreas' meeting with Gotthilff at the village inn in Villach has about it the sinister air of an encounter with a malign fate. Presenting himself to Andreas with dramatic, even offensive, urgency, the servant appears to be already familiar with Andreas' name as well as with the probable location of Andreas' money: "Should he go down and . . . fetch the saddle? There was undoubtedly a fortune in ducats sewn up inside" (E, 124). The following morning, before Andreas is even awake, Gotthilff is standing at the door again, and Andreas, "before he really knew it or wanted it," finds that he has acquired a traveling companion. Not only is Gotthilff's attachment to Andreas unavoidable, but his very character has about it an element of tragic necessity. His name (God-helper), like that of Lucifer (Light-bearer) or even like such German euphemisms for the devil as "Gottseibeiuns" (God be with us), appears to be an ironic hint at his hidden origin and necessary role in life—an irony not uncommon in Hofmannsthal, who also gave the less than impeccable servant in Der Unbestechliche the name Theodor (God's gift). For when viewed from the standpoint of Andreas' overall development, Gotthilff might be deemed a Mephistophelian servant, one who, although constantly bent on evil, unwittingly effects an eventual good. As Hofmannsthal points out in the important "Briefe des Zurückgekehrten" of the same year, even horse thieves can possess a wholeness of being. "There is a devoutness in life," he explains, "and it can be found in a hard, grudging, niggardly peasant, and even in a ruthless villain of a horse thief" (PII, 292).

At the opposite pole from Gotthilff (and the maid to

whom he attaches himself, "a wench," as he tells Andreas, "not from these parts, but from down the valley" [E, 140]) stands the world of the Finazzerhof. In fact, so peaceful and serene is this landscape that several critics have been led to speak of it in terms of an earthly paradise: a *heile Welt*, concealing within it "traces of Paradise," one has termed it, and another has found it directly reminiscent of the "sacred landscapes of Stifter," a landscape in which "good . . . is self-evident" and in which the Finazzers, like all true country people, "live in a timeless fashion."[17] Actually, however, the Finazzerhof is as little the incarnation of an earthly paradise as Gotthilff, on the other hand, is an embodiment of absolute evil. To maintain that it is, is to overlook Romana's first words to Andreas: " 'Do you have to while away the time?' " she asks him, " 'It passes quickly enough for me; often I'm afraid' " (E, 132), as well as the fact that death is no less absent from the surroundings than are life and beauty: six of Romana's younger brothers and sisters died in childhood and now lie in the graveyard behind the village church, where she faithfully tends their graves. Nor is the darker side missing from her vision of the afterlife; at the farm she earnestly shows Andreas a book of the seven deadly sins, explaining "how each punishment precisely fits its sin" (E, 135). Time, death, and suffering for the Finazzers are a very real part of everyday life.

The pattern of the first day's events, which reflects the developing love between Andreas and Romana, begins with the brightness and peace of the afternoon scenes in the village churchyard and culminates in the disaster that night. The symbolic progression, which mirrors Andreas' own vicarious descent into darkness and sin, revolves around three bedroom scenes. The first occurs in Andreas' room, scene of the lovers' first embrace; the second, in Romana's

[17] Hederer, p. 268; Gautschi, pp. 39-40.

own bedroom, portrays the defeat of Andreas' dreams of consummating their love; and the last, which takes place in the bedroom of the maid in the early hours of the morning, brings the final calamity. The first is effectively framed by two contrasting encounters with Gotthilff in the stables. Andreas and Romana, returning from their afternoon walk to the cemetery, suddenly surprise Gotthilff and the maid in the darkness: "Entering the stables they came upon the young servant-girl crouching by the fire, her hair hanging in wisps over her flushed cheeks, the servant more on top of her than beside her. . . . 'Shall I add more saltpeter,' said the girl, tittering" (E, 138). Andreas, shocked and embarrassed, abruptly orders the servant to carry the luggage to his room, but his demand is ignored and Andreas is forced to carry it himself, followed by Romana. In his room, in vivid contrast to the dark, animal sensuality of the previous scene, and on a bed decorated with the designs of saints and flowers, Andreas exchanges his first kiss with Romana; but he soon returns to the stables, this time alone, and in so doing almost collides with Gotthilff in the deepening gloom. Moreover, a salacious remark of the servant's conjures up frightening images in Andreas' mind. "He saw Romana in her nightgown, sitting on her virgin bed in the dark, with her bare feet drawn up under her, staring at the door-latch. She had pointed out her door to him as well as the empty room next to it, and had talked about her bed—it all passed before his eyes like mountain mist" (E, 140). Both repelled and confused by the vision, Andreas turns and leaves the stalls abruptly.

Just as the scene of Andreas' and Romana's first embrace is contrasted with the events in the stables, so their second meeting is framed by Andreas' naive dreams of marital happiness with Romana. Before he goes to her bedroom that night, he accidentally overhears her parents discussing his relationship with their daughter in simple, reassuring tones, and is filled with confidence: "He said to himself, one day this will be my house and my wife; then I shall lie beside her, talking about our children. Now he was sure that she was waiting for him in the same mood as he was going to her, waiting for warm, innocent embraces and a secret betrothal" (E, 143). His hope is short-lived, however, for he discovers one of the maids sleeping next to Romana; yet when once more back in his own room, he continues to dream of their happy future together. In an imaginary letter to his parents, he fantasizes about his future bliss: "Now through God's sudden dispensation he had found the girl, his life-long companion, who would guarantee his happiness. From now on he had only *one* object in mind: to make his parents happy through his own happiness at the side of this girl" (E, 145).

The unconscious tension in Andreas' feelings for Romana comes to a head in a more symbolic, vicarious fashion in the third and final bedroom scene. The event is once again anticipated by contrast, for Andreas has just seen himself in a dream pursuing Romana through the crowded streets of Vienna near his home. To reach her in the dream he must, however, first find his way past the writhing body of a cat in the doorway (a cat he had killed many years ago as a boy), and, just as he manages to raise his heavy foot over the animal and is proceeding to fight his way through his parents' clothes-closet to aid the screaming Romana, he suddenly awakes. The dream obviously re-enacts, in condensed, symbolic form, the unconscious dilemma in Andreas' relationship to Romana, the deepening conflict between a desperate fear of sex and an almost obsessive desire for marriage and children. Social tensions also add to Andreas' psychological problems: in the dream he is chasing Romana through the city streets of Vienna, near his home;

she herself, fleeing before him, is strangely dressed, "half as peasant-girl, half as lady, barefoot under her pleated, black brocade skirt" (E, 145). In addition, there still stand in his way both a deep sense of guilt (reflected in his mistreatment of the cat) and an unresolved past (the closet of undiscarded clothes).

The dream, moreover, merges in uncanny fashion with reality, for upon awakening Andreas is not freed from his sense of guilt but is actually oppressed even more by it; he feels "like a condemned man, awakened by the call of the hangman," and the screams of the terrified maid from downstairs strike his ears as if they issued "from the damned in hell." When he arrives on the scene, he hears from the maid's lips nothing but the screams of terror "for a just God to hear her," and the fervent prayers "to forgive her her terrible sin." He suddenly notices Romana there as well, cowering "half-dressed, barefoot, and trembling" in a doorway. "Almost as I saw her in my dream, something said inside him. When she noticed him, an expression of infinite horror crossed her face." And later, when Andreas questions a young farmhand about the incident, he feels as if he is "covered with blood before the lad's honest face" (E, 147-149).

Although Andreas' "sin" is largely vicarious (reflected in Gotthilff and the maid) and in the past (in the childhood memories of the animal he had tortured and killed), it is no less real. His dream and the ensuing scenes not only suggest past and present repressions but reflect an anxiety towards the future as well. Furthermore, the fact that he should become conscious of his love for Romana at the very moment when his guilt feelings reach a peak is also important, for his love for her must first recognize and transcend its darker side (as portrayed in Gotthilff and the servant-girl) before it can be consummated—a fact hinted at in the notes, where we learn that Andreas is "on the one hand attracted to the sensual, on the other to the ideal" (E, 222). This interdependence of Gotthilff and Romana is, moreover, emphasized by the very structure of the plot, for Andreas, in a sense, is actually led to Romana by Gotthilff. Not only is it the spirited little Finazzer horse presented by Gotthilff that originally arouses Andreas' visions of travelling in grand style, but it is also the servant who selects their travel route, and whose lame (Finazzer) horse forces them to turn in at the Finazzer estate. And in the end on leaving the Finazzerhof, Andreas must retrace the route to Villach where he originally met Gotthilff before he can continue on his way to Venice. The entire episode, both realistically and symbolically, follows the pattern of a circle, one in which Gotthilff plays as vital a role as do Romana and the Finazzers.

Andreas as "Sick Soul": The Ethics of Evil
(The Second Day)

If Andreas' first day acquaints him with the polarities of life in the figures of Romana and Gotthilff, his second day convinces him of their necessary interdependence. On the second morning, in contrast to the previous day's world of black-and-white extremes, he awakens to a landscape of monotonous grey. "The clouds hung motionless over and into the valley, everything was overcast and heavy, as desolate as the end of the world" (E, 151). Left alone with his conscience, Andreas spends most of the day reflecting upon himself and the past, rather than on others and the future as he had done the previous day, and his thoughts are haunted above all by a deep and tragic sense of guilt.

The question of guilt in *Andreas* has generally been overlooked by critics, perhaps because many of them have tended to view Andreas' development as a progression following the simple, two-stage scheme outlined in *Ad me ipsum*—from the innocence of pre-existence to the trials of existence. Alewyn, for example, sees Andreas as simply another of Hofmannsthal's youthful heroes, "standing at the threshold of life (in the dangerous and ambiguous position between pre-existence and existence, to use the language of *Ad me ipsum*)."[18] Gautschi describes Andreas as having lost his "absolute connection with the cosmos" at an early age: "However, Andreas, although still deeply rooted in pre-existence, is eager to find the path into real life. He is thus following the advice given in *Ad me ipsum*. His development shows a close connection with Hofmannsthal's own 'self-interpretation'; one could almost speak of a realization of the theory."[19]

The danger of resorting to the terms of pre-existence and existence to explain Andreas' development, as we have already mentioned, is that such a passage from innocence to experience characterizes in a general fashion practically all processes of maturation. Furthermore, there is not a single reference in the fragment to a period of blissful innocence in Andreas' childhood; the closest instance is perhaps a moment at the theater when he was twelve, but even here the experience was more ambiguous than euphoric, for it is described as the feeling of a "double-edged sword [which] had pierced his soul, . . . of the most exquisite delight and unspeakable longing to the point of tears, awe, and ecstasy" (E, 121). On the contrary, Andreas' memories of childhood are filled with an overpowering sense of unhappiness and guilt. Two experiences in particular continue to plague him: as a young child he had killed a cat by striking at it with a wagon axle, and again, when he was twelve, he had broken his dog's back by kicking at it. The two

[18] Alewyn, *Über Hugo von Hofmannsthal*, p. 144.
[19] Gautschi, p. 31.

moments of cruelty, however, are somewhat blurred in his memory; in fact, "he was not sure whether he had done it or not" (E, 155).

Yet the insight gained by Andreas from these memories involves far more than what Gautschi terms the "infinite power of the glance" in the animal's eye,[20] for a particular image in the description of both incidents lends the memories a far deeper significance. In the first instance, the dying cat edges towards Andreas "creeping . . . like a snake" (E, 146) and again, in the second, the small dog crawls after his master "like a snake, his legs giving way under him with each step" (E, 155). In the eyes of Andreas, in other words, the dying animal transforms itself in both cases into a writhing snake—the time-honored symbol of sin, in particular of original sin. The image, whose symbolic nature is further emphasized by the fact that at one point the violent memories of the dog and the cat merge into the grotesque head of a creature "at once cat and dog" (E, 146), points to a yet deeper dimension in the meaning of Andreas' suffering and guilt.

Andreas' susceptibility to such deep feelings of sin and melancholia on his second day at the Finazzerhof borders on the pathological; moreover, as we know from the notes, he also suffers from "touches of anhedonia" (E, 221). His temperament, in fact, is strikingly similar to that of the "sick soul" as described by William James in *The Varieties of Religious Experience* (1902)—a work that exercised a profound effect on Hofmannsthal's conception of *Andreas*.[21] According to the many annotations and markings in his own copy, Hofmannsthal apparently read James's chapter on "The Reality of the Unseen" in 1908, when he himself was confessedly "physically and spiritually sick," and in the fol-

[20] *Ibid.*, p. 27.
[21] See Alewyn, *Über Hugo von Hofmannsthal*, p. 160.

lowing year he went on to read the chapters "The Sick Soul" and "Conversion."[22] All three chapters have a strong bearing on the ultimate meaning of Andreas' experiences of guilt and suffering within the overall pattern of his process of Bildung.

The sick soul, a term that James very possibly drew from *Hamlet*[23] and that he contrasts to the "healthy-minded," suffers above all from fits of melancholia and pathological depression bordering on anhedonia. (The latter concept Hofmannsthal undoubtedly borrowed directly from James, who in turn took it from Ribot; formed analogously to *analgesia*, insensibility to pain, it refers to an insensibility to pleasure, to hedonistic joys.) Such a person is moreover "so choked with the feeling of evil that the sense of there being any good in the world is lost for him altogether." Yet, as James is careful to point out, this overpowering sense of sin can lead to a deeper understanding of the world than is ever possible for the healthy-minded: "The happiness that comes, when any does come," he writes, "is not the simple ignorance of ill, but something vastly more complex, including natural evil as one of its elements, but finding natural evil no such stumbling-block and terror because it now sees it swallowed up in supernatural good. The process," James concludes, "is one of redemption, not of mere reversion to natural health, and the sufferer, when saved, is saved by what seems to him a second birth, a deeper kind of conscious being than he could enjoy before." Moreover, the evil aspects of the world, which the sick soul refuses to overlook, constitute, in James's words, "a genuine portion of

---

[22] Michael Hamburger, "Hofmannsthals Bibliothek," *Euphorion*, 55 (1961), 29.

[23] Cf. the Queen's aside in IV, v:

> To my sick soul (as sin's true nature is)
> Each toy seems prologue to some great amiss.

reality; and they may after all be the best key to life's significance, and possibly the only openers of our own eyes to the deepest levels of truth."[24]

When relief does come to the "morbid-minded," as James terms them, it brings with it a knowledge of deeper religious truths. This is, in fact, precisely what happens to Andreas on the afternoon of the second day. His sense of guilt, intensified by repeated thoughts of the dog he had killed, suddenly penetrates to a deeper sphere, where the numbing pain mingles with a strange measure of yearning: "He was touched by the infinite. The memory was torture, yet a wave of nostalgia welled up inside him for the twelve-year-old Andreas who had done this deed" (E, 155). Somewhat later, after having thrown himself in despair on the fresh grave of the Finazzer dog, he has the sudden vision of a deeper reality that does not exclude suffering and guilt: "There was something between him and the dead dog—he didn't know what—just as there was something between him and Gotthilff, who was to blame for the animal's death, and on the other hand between this dog and the one of his childhood. All these connections ran to and fro, weaving a world which was beyond the real world and far less empty and desolate" (E, 156).

Andreas' key memories, much like his distressing dream-visions on the first night at the Finazzerhof, not only provide symbolic images of his inner turmoil, but also represent the unconscious attempt on his part to accept certain painful moments in the past. He is often assailed by memories of "childhood dreams frequently dreamed to the point of disgust" (E, 189), for instance, and in the notes we read that "in the memories of childhood there remains a painful complexity, something that an entire lifetime could

[24] William James, *The Varieties of Religious Experience* (New York, Modern Library), pp. 146, 153-154, and 160.

scarcely resolve" (E, 222). Andreas' greatest desire is simply "to die reconciled with his childhood" (E, 222). This compulsion to remember also characterizes his recollection of the Finazzerhof incidents: "Whether he wanted to or not, he was compelled to recall everything in minute detail from the very beginning: and so it happened, once a day, morning or evening" (E, 122). The process actually seems to foreshadow an insight of Freud's of some years later. For Andreas, much like Freud's compulsive child in "Beyond the Pleasure Principle" (1920), appears to be rehearsing (in his mind, in this case) the painful events of the past in an unconscious attempt to master them. As he is informed by Sacramozo, one must come to affirm, "from one's present standpoint, the chain of [past] experiences as necessary" (E, 244). Thus the compulsive recurrence of these memories, including the memory of his sudden vision at the dog's grave of a world "beyond the real world," indicates that Andreas is gradually moving towards a deeper awareness of the necessity of death and suffering in the world (E, 156). Like James's sick soul, he must come to understand the "experience of evil as something essential." For morbid-mindedness, ranging over the "wider scale of experience," as James observes, does not relegate death and evil to a lesser reality, but views them as being ultimately absorbed into the deeper design of life as a whole.[25]

Andreas' process of Bildung, then, is to be one not of steady maturation but rather of recovery and rebirth, much as after a mortal illness. To overstate the point, whereas Wilhelm Meister's Bildung is a phenomenon of growth (however haphazard this may be), Andreas' is one of convalescence. In this respect he is similar to other heroes of the modern Bildungsroman, who in general tend to be more of the sick-souled variety than the healthy-minded. Rilke's

[25] James, *Varieties*, pp. 159-160.

Malte, for instance, wallowing in his *Kranksein*, craves above all to be a liberated soul like Bettina von Arnim, who projected herself so deeply into existence that she lived "as if she were after her death."[26] And even such a middling hero as Hans Castorp, aided by the numbing, white transcendence of an Alpine snowstorm, envisions at one point a dream-poem of humanity in which goodness and love exist not apart from, but rather on the far side of, blood-sacrifice. As Mann explains to us, what Castorp "comes to understand is that one must go through the deep experience of sickness and death to arrive at a higher sanity and health; in just the same way that one must have a knowledge of sin in order to find redemption."[27] Much like the sick soul, Castorp takes the second of the two paths of life, which, as Mann puts it, is the path of all genius and which first subjects the soul to the long night and to death before bringing it to wisdom and knowledge.[28]

The world beyond,[29] then, that Andreas discovers within

[26] Rainer Maria Rilke, *Sämtliche Werke* (Frankfurt a. M., 1966), VI, 897. This theme of the vital interdependence of death and life occurs in many variations in Rilke. Thus Malte's grandfather tends to confuse the living with the dead; the angels in the first of the *Duino Elegies* often cannot distinguish whether they are moving in the realm of life or of death; and Orpheus, in the ninth of the *Sonnets to Orpheus*, is also connected with this "double realm."

[27] Thomas Mann, "The Making of *The Magic Mountain*" in *The Magic Mountain*, trans. H. T. Lowe-Porter (New York, Modern Library), pp. 724-725.

[28] Theodore Ziolkowski, who in his *Dimensions of the Modern Novel* (Princeton, 1969) studies the role of death in Rilke, Mann, and several other writers, makes the interesting observation that the modern writer, in rejecting both the classical humanist's radical emphasis on life and the romanticist's longing for transcendence in death, actually celebrates an awareness of death *within* life, a form of *immanent* transcendence (see pp. 215-257).

[29] "Eine Welt, die hinter der wirklichen war" (E, 156), a phrase reminiscent of the *Zurückgekehrter*, who discovers a deeper reality

himself on his second day at the Finazzerhof, refers, together with the infinite that is revealed to him in his memory of the suffering dog, to that level of reality envisioned by both Malte and Hans Castorp, namely to the level where "natural evil," in James's words, "is swallowed up in the supernatural good." It is the point where the extremes of existence meet, where the lines of life's antinomies converge in a deeper awareness. In Venice Andreas experiences this same sense of the infinite when he perceives within Maria's personality the traces of her darker self Mariquita, the sensual *within* the spiritual. "And in this moment Andreas senses that he will never know this woman, and feels that here Infinity has touched him with a sharper pang than any pain he has ever known"; in fact, Andreas has "three or four memories that bear within them this 'sharp point of infinity' " (E, 204).[30] In each case, however, although the intuited realm connects with the infinite, the experience is essentially one of an *immanent* transcendence, which incorporates the sick soul's "deeper kind of conscious being" but which has no need of a specific religious interpretation.

in art—"das, was hinter dem Gemalten war" (PII, 302)—as well as in life—"dies Wirkliche hinter dem Alltäglichen" (PII, 296).

[30] The actual phrase Hofmannsthal uses here is the French "pointe acérée de l'infini" (the "sharp point of infinity"), a favorite line of Hofmannsthal's, which he had taken from Baudelaire's prose poem "Le *Confiteor* de l'Artiste." (See also [A, 233], for instance.) Hofmannsthal quotes the fuller context in his notebooks (in French): "There are certain sensations of delight whose vagueness does not exclude intensity, and there is no sharper point than that of the infinite" (A, 181-182). Although Baudelaire himself is referring in the poem chiefly to the sensation of infinity occasioned by certain seasons and landscapes (such as the vastness of the sea, the silent immensity of the sky, and the penetrating quality of autumnal evenings), Hofmannsthal seems to use the phrase in a more metaphorical sense, equating the sensation with the penetrating quality of certain memories. In his essay "Erinnerung," for instance, he can use it to describe the sharp onslaught of memories often preceding a period of artistic creation (PIV, 206).

The intense feeling in each case is related not to a religious absolute but to the infinity of life itself. The spiritual relief that awaits Andreas will eventually come about not through the agency of divine grace in a Christian sense but rather through the idealization of a secular love. And this love finds its beginnings in Andreas' brief but highly significant encounter with Romana.

Romana and Ideal Love: A Parallel to *La Vita Nuova* (The Third Day)

> Die Begegnung verspricht mehr, als die Umarmung halten kann. Sie scheint, wenn ich so sagen darf, einer höheren Ordnung der Dinge anzugehören, jener, nach der die Sterne sich bewegen. . . . Dante datiert sein "Neues Leben" von einem Gruss, der ihm zuteil geworden.
>
> (PII, 266)

OF THE central questions posed by *Andreas* in its fragmentary form, one of the most vexing concerns the very title itself. What, exactly, does Hofmannsthal mean by *Die Vereinigten*? The words, which form an obvious counterpoint to Goethe's *Die Entsagenden* (the subtitle of his second volume on Wilhelm Meister), could refer either to Andreas' eventual recovery—to the reintegration of his desperately divided self—or to his reunion with Romana. When we consider the ending of the first volume of Goethe's Bildungsroman, for instance, with its happy tableau of united lovers, there would seem to be little doubt that the title refers to the relationship between Andreas and Romana (particularly when we recall that the theme of the separated lovers has been a standby of novelistic form since the earliest beginnings of the genre). However, even if we assume that the *Vereinigung* refers to *all* possible combinations in the novel, that is, to the relationship between each character and his own alter ego (as between "Maria" and

"Mariquita"),[31] to that between Andreas and Romana, *and* to that of all the figures to one another, we are still left with the deeper psychological problem of what precisely is meant by *Vereinigung*. As Sacramozo puts it to Andreas, "In what does union with another human being consist? In understanding? In possessing?" or, in a possible hint at Andreas' own case, "In the first meeting?" (E, 238)

Critics have tended to differ on this point. Whereas Alewyn, for example, assumes the eventual reunion of Andreas with Romana, Gautschi views this as highly improbable, asserting that Andreas' failure to win her is the more likely ending.[32] What I would like to suggest, however, is that neither of these endings to the novel is very likely but that the ultimate answer for Andreas will lie rather in the realm of some unattainable, idealized form of love. This would be an ending that would accord, for instance, with the spirit of the last note to the novel, that "with Romana," as Andreas says to himself, "heaven might be mine."[33] Moreover, this interpretation would also help to bring out the significance of the novel's obscure epigraph, which consists of two lines from Ariosto's *Orlando Furioso*, a work that is given to Andreas by Sacramozo in order that he may learn of the miraculous world of poetry contained therein, a world lying above and beyond that of nature, and conquering all time (E, 201, 228):

Es hat in unsrer Mitte Zauberer
Und Zauberinnen, aber niemand weiss sie.

(VIII, 1-2)

---

[31] See the unpublished note cited by Alewyn in his *Über Hugo von Hofmannsthal*: "Die Vereinigten—auch auf die Subjekte selber bezogen: Andres—Marie—der Malteser, für jeden geht es um das Eins-werden mit sich selber" (p. 191, n. 70).

[32] Alewyn, *Über Hugo von Hofmannsthal*, p. 144; Gautschi, p. 97.

[33] (E, 247): "Mit Romana, sagt er sich, könnte es sein Himmel sein."

The lines, which in the novel allude to the figure of Maria and thus, by extension, to Romana as well, refer expressly to the magic of courtly love.[34]

On the first day of Andreas' visit to the Finazzerhof, the tragic antinomies of life are bodied forth for him in the figures of the Finazzers as well as in those of Gotthilff and the maid, and on the second he is granted the redemptive vision of a world beyond in which the ultimate unity of these polarities would seem to lie. On the third day, however, he becomes aware that this world beyond may somehow tie in with his love for Romana through the gradual sublimation of his erotic memory of her into an ideal vision. This solution would actually include, rather than exclude, the suggestions of both Alewyn and Gautschi, for Andreas would be united with Romana, but not in a physical sense. Of the several indications in the text that Romana may perhaps become a spiritual ideal for Andreas, by far the most significant occurs in a scene in Andreas' bedroom on the morning of his last day at the Finazzerhof. The scene, in fact, is so very strange that it is difficult to understand why not a single critic has commented upon it.

Directly preceding the scene, which opens with Andreas' being awakened by a sound at his window, he has an extraordinary dream, one which is important enough for us to consider briefly before proceeding to the scene itself. (The dream, indicating a symbolic juncture or turning point in the life of the *Bildungsheld*, is also present, interestingly enough, in both *Wilhelm Meister* [VII, 1] and *Der grüne Heinrich* [2nd version, IV, 6-7].) As on the previous night, Andreas dreams of Romana. "The sun was shining, he went deeper and deeper into the tall forest, and found Romana. The deeper he went into the wood, the brighter

---

[34] See also (LIII, 396), where the same quotation is used in connection with the magic of love in *Danae*.

it shone: in the middle, where everything was darkest and most radiant, he found her sitting on a little island meadow around which shining water flowed. She had fallen asleep haymaking, her sickle and rake beside her. As he stepped over the water, she looked up at him, but as she might at a stranger" (E, 157). The landscape of the dream suggests very clearly that of an earthly paradise. As has been shown by Giamatti in an important study of this topic in literature, the earthly paradise had been portrayed, from the time of antiquity through the Renaissance, as a "safe place across the water,"[35] and Romana here is located in a meadow surrounded by a luminous stream. Similarly, in Ariosto's *Orlando Furioso* the terrestrial paradise is located beyond a crystal stream (Canto XXXII), just as in Dante's *Purgatorio* it is situated in an ancient wood across a stream of purest water (Canto XXVIII).

Yet Hofmannsthal, who was indeed familiar with both Dante and Ariosto, would not necessarily have had to have read these particular writers to have found inspirations for his own scene. The German Bildungsroman, a much closer tradition, also contains references to the same phenomenon. For the topos of the paradisal garden, or "garden of love,"[36] occurs in slightly modified form in the novels of both Novalis and Hölderlin. At the end of the sixth chapter of *Heinrich von Ofterdingen*, for instance, the youthful medieval hero Heinrich has a dream of his beloved (who

[35] A. Bartlett Giamatti, *The Earthly Paradise and the Renaissance Epic* (Princeton, 1966), p. 104.

[36] I am referring here to the set piece of classical landscape description, the *locus amoenus*, whose history has been traced by E. R. Curtius, among others. See his *European Literature and the Latin Middle Ages*, trans. W. R. Trask (Princeton, 1953), p. 192, 195 ff. As Giamatti points out (*The Earthly Paradise*, p. 34, n. 35), Curtius shows how Servius connected *amoenus* with *amor* and thus gave rise to the topos of the "love-ly place": the pleasant place *and* a place for love.

139

is called, like the figure in Dante's paradise, Mathilde) that is very similar to Andreas': he must first cross a deep blue stream shining in a green plain, and beyond this—or rather, beneath it—he must press deeper and deeper into a land of trees and flowers until he finally discovers Mathilde, who informs him that they are in the land of their fathers. And in the last letter of Hölderlin's Bildungsroman *Hyperion*, the hero describes how he had been in a paradisal spot, by the waters of a spring, in the protective shade of blooming bushes and ivy, when he had suddenly been overcome by a dream-like vision of Diotima in which she had informed him that she was now in the land of their parents.

Andreas' dream, however, is decidedly different from those of both Heinrich and Hyperion. For the island meadow of Romana is obviously a paradise to which he does not yet belong. Not only does Romana stare at him as at a stranger, totally failing to recognize him, but she also confuses him with the evil Gotthilff, who had poisoned her dog. "He called to her, 'Romana, can you see me?' Her eyes were so vacant. 'Why, yes, of course,' she said, with a strange look. 'Do you know, I don't know where the dog is buried'. . . . He was close to her and felt that she believed him to be the wicked Gotthilff, and yet not Gotthilff either, and he himself was not quite sure who he was. She implored him not to tie her naked to the bed in front of all the people, and not to run away on a stolen horse." The dream closes, moreover, with yet another scene of failure on Andreas' part when he again comes upon Romana, sensuous and radiant, in a different part of the wood: "And she came to meet him between two beautiful maples, as gay and friendly as if nothing had happened. Her eyes shone with a strange radiance, her bare feet were luminous on the moss, and the hem of her dress was wet. 'What kind of woman are you?' he cried in wonder. 'This kind,' she said, holding up her mouth to him. As he stretched out his arms to embrace her, 'What sort of a man are you!' she cried, striking at him with her rake. She hit him on the forehead, there was a sharp, clear sound as if a pane of glass had broken. He awoke with a start."

Upon awakening, Andreas senses that the dream has been a form of revelation. Whereas the previous night's dreams had centered on the disturbing images of Romana running through Vienna and of the suffering cat barring Andreas' way to her, his present dream pictures her in a paradisal haying meadow in the Alps (although his way to her is still blocked by memories of guilt and evil—the dead Finazzer dog that is on his conscience—and by his uncertainty as to his own identity). Moreover, the figure of Romana has changed as well: no longer incongruously barefoot in city streets, she now appears as a doe-like figure merging with the soft moss of the garden of love. And as is clear from the imagery, this love, as is usually the case in the earthly paradise, is as sensual as it is spiritual. Whereas on the previous night Romana had clearly embodied Andreas' frustrated longing for marriage, children, and bourgeois comforts, she now seems to promise a future love and joy that would completely transcend the tangible and the mundane. Although Andreas realizes, upon awakening, that these visions were only dreams, he senses in them a truth that fills him with a deep joy: "Romana's whole being had been revealed to him with a vividness that was above reality. All heaviness was gone. Within him or without, he could not lose her. He had the knowledge, moreover, the faith, that she lived for him. He returned to the world like one blessed" (E, 158).

Still half-dreaming, Andreas goes over to the window to seek the cause of the noise that had awakened him. Yet instead of finding Romana calling to him from outside, he discovers a crack in the windowpane and a dead bird on the window sill. Picking up the bird Andreas carries it slowly back to his bed and in a state of wonder lays it on his pillow. "The small body poured delight through his very veins; he felt as if he could easily have restored the bird to life if he had simply held it to his heart. He sat on the bed with a thousand thoughts streaming through his head: he was happy. His body was a temple inhabited by Romana's soul, and passing time flowed around him and lapped at the steps of the temple" (E, 158). This extraordinary scene, with its strange image of the fallen bird and its vision of the timeless temple of love, tells us much about the future of Andreas' love for Romana. On the most obvious level, the episode represents a sort of turning point, a moment in which Andreas, suffering from those indispositions of the mind and soul that William James termed a true "sickness," first recognizes in Romana the possibility not of marriage, but of something much deeper: the promise of a rebirth through ideal love. This idea is further supported, in a manner much less obvious, by the strange symbol of the dead bird, an image so striking as to suggest a parallel to one of the world's most famous poems on love and rebirth— namely, Dante's *Vita Nuova*.

La Vita Nuova, we recall, is Dante's spiritual autobiography, a work that celebrates, in both poetry and prose, his Beatrice experience, the encounter that eventually opened his eyes to the "new life" and effected his initiation into that mystical theology of love that would later inform the *Divine Comedy*. The book could almost, in fact, be termed a form of confessional (although highly spiritualized) Bildungsroman, for it faithfully records the sufferings and experiences of his own development from the age of nine to approximately thirty. The experiences center on his gradual sublimation of a youthful earthly passion into a divine and idealized one, into a form of *caritas*; in short, it portrays the mystical transfiguration of Beatrice into a beatific redeemer. The deep mysticism of their first encounter, when both of them were only nine years old, is in fact described by Hofmannsthal himself at one point, in one of his early dramas. (The particular dream referred to by Hofmannsthal here actually occurred nine years *after* the encounter.)

> ... und der Dichter Dante [war]
> neun Jahr, als ihm der Liebesgott im Traum
> erschien und in Sonetten zu ihm sprach!
> Die Seele hat kein Alter . . . .   (DI, 261)

Strangely enough, however, the central experience of Dante's new life concerns neither his first glimpse of Beatrice nor the first greeting, but rather his prophetic vision of her death. At the very midpoint of the work—in the twenty-third chapter and the following canzone—he describes the experience. On the ninth day of an illness so severe as to turn his thoughts toward death, he is struck for the first time in his life by the sudden awareness that Beatrice, too, must die some day. In a fever-heightened dream, he imagines that he sees her in a strange merging of daylight and darkness. Much as Andreas in his dream finds the *radiant* Romana in the middle of a *dark* wood and awakens to discover the dead bird, Dante imagines that there is a darkening of the sun, that stars appear, and that at this precise moment the very birds flying through the air fall dead to earth. Following this, he has a vision of Beatrice's soul being borne aloft amidst flights of angels, and he then awakens from the "realistic dream" saying "O Beatrice, blessed art thou." In the following canzone, we learn that the vision of the dying birds has exercised a powerful effect

143

on his imagination, for he mentions the very same image once again (in what is actually the central canzone of the entire work):

> It seemed to me that then I saw the sun
> Grow slowly darker and a star appear,
> And sun and star did weep;
> The birds that fly above fell dead to earth.[37]

That the imagery of *Andreas* should incorporate a parallel to that of the *Vita Nuova* is not as strange nor as far-fetched as it might at first appear. By the age of fifteen, at the latest, Hofmannsthal had read Dante in the original,[38] and at the University of Vienna, of course, he had studied Romance philology. It is also possible that the poet came into contact with Dante through his associations with various members of the George-circle. Both George and Rudolf Borchardt, for example, were translators of Dante, and one of Hofmannsthal's poems is even entitled "Nach einer Dante-Lektüre." Most likely of all, however, is that Hofmannsthal had discovered Dante through his knowledge and appreciation of the English Pre-Raphaelites, whose movement was characterized in particular by an emphasis on the *Vita Nuova* and a cult of the Beatrician image of love. The twenty-year-old Hofmannsthal, for instance, in reporting on an international exhibition of paintings in Vienna, notes how much the Pre-Raphaelite movement, beginning, characteristically, with *Dante* Gabriel Rossetti, had schooled it-

---

[37] Citations from Dante in my text are to *La Vita Nuova*, trans. M. Musa (Bloomington, 1965). It is interesting to speculate whether Dante's imagery was in turn influenced in part by the striking image in the New Testament that a sparrow itself "shall not fall on the ground without your Father" (Matt. 10:29), a phrase that also appealed to Shakespeare, who writes in *Hamlet* (V, ii) that "there's a special providence in the fall of a sparrow."

[38] Volke, p. 17.

self in the literary visions of Dante. For it was Beatrice, he remarks, "and other women with mystic eyes and slender hands," who "became the subject of their paintings" (PI, 197). Comparing the literary images of the *Vita Nuova* to those in paintings, Hofmannsthal also points to the relationship between Beatrice and primitive portraits of the Madonna.[39]

Elsewhere in Hofmannsthal's writings, Dante is mentioned in connection with the "grand style" of his works (A, 199f.), with his "immense architectonics" (PII, 148), and with his truly Homeric vision (PII, 276). Yet beyond these and other comments, there exists an even more pertinent reference to Dante in the book of a close friend of Hofmannsthal's—the study *Die Mystik, die Künstler und das Leben* by Rudolf Kassner, a work Hofmannsthal was so taken with that he read it in one sitting. In his chapter on Dante Gabriel Rossetti, Kassner notes precisely that scene in the *Vita Nuova* we have been referring to: "Because of her," he writes, referring to Beatrice, Dante "experienced those wonderful visions in the *Vita Nuova* . . . of the death of his beloved when . . . the birds fell dead to earth."[40]

That for Hofmannsthal the imagery of birds in general could connect with the concept of spiritual love is also hinted at in his impressionistic essay "Die Wege und die Begegnungen." Composed in 1907 (the same year *Andreas* was begun), this piece is written in a prose whose lyricism and imagery relate it directly to the novel. The poet begins the essay by evoking what are to him life's two greatest wonders (referred to in the title): the miracle of the path-

[39] In the same year (May, 1894), in a letter to Elsa Bruckmann-Cantacuzene, Hofmannsthal asks, with reference to the importance of Dante, whether or not she is well acquainted with the *Vita Nuova* in particular (BI, 102).

[40] Rudolf Kassner, *Die Mystik, die Künstler und das Leben* (Leipzig, 1900), p. 151.

ways of birds in flight and the mystery of the encounter of love. In a reference to Proverbs (30:18-19)—"There be . . . things which are too wonderful for me, yea . . . which I know not: The way of an eagle in the air . . . and the way of a man with a maid"—he quotes a passage in French, yet with an important variation: "Je me souviens des paroles d'Agur . . . et des choses qu'il déclare les plus incompréhensibles et les plus merveilleuses: la trace de l'oiseau dans l'air et la trace de l'homme dans la *vierge*" (PII, 264; italics mine). The reason for the alteration from maid to virgin soon becomes evident, however, for the love encounters Hofmannsthal is describing here, like the one portrayed in *Andreas*, are those that embody a mystical blend of the erotic and the spiritual.

The pathways of migratory birds, in other words, become for Hofmannsthal a sensuous cipher of the world of the spirit, a world that can also manifest itself through the momentary encounter of two human beings. "It appears to me," he writes, that "the actually decisive erotic pantomime is not the embrace, but the encounter" (PII, 265). The encounter, for a poetic imagination, can promise more than the real embrace can ever hold, and in this promise, as Hofmannsthal puts it, is the hint of a divine order lying beyond the earth and moving the very stars. The secret of the ways of birds and the secret of love's ways are, in their deepest sense, the same. The images with which Hofmannsthal portrays the encounter of love in the essay remind us directly of *Andreas*, where Romana, in the dream, is like a doe and yet somehow connected with the darker realms represented by Gotthilff and the poisoned dog; for embodied in the encounter there is a "yearning for one another that is still without lust—a naive combination of intimacy and shyness. In such is the doe-like, the bird-like, the darkly animalistic, the angelic, the divine. In a greeting there are infinite possibilities. Dante dates his *New Life* from a greeting bestowed on him" (PII, 265-266).[41]

Although all of these many references to Dante in Hofmannsthal's writings and experiences make it indeed very likely that the scene in *Andreas* is modelled on that in the *Vita Nuova*, it should be stressed that this was not necessarily a conscious attempt on Hofmannsthal's part at symbolic prefiguration. On the contrary, from what we know of Hofmannsthal's enormous range of reading and his almost eidetic memory, it is very likely that the parallel was largely an unconscious one; moreover, it is possible that in later drafts the image might have been either expanded or even totally removed. Yet this we can never know, and as it stands, the parallel in an image so striking and unusual is impossible to overlook. Moreover, Andreas' experiences with Romana on this last day of his stay lead us to very similar conclusions. After his discovery of the bird, Andreas— sensing that "wherever he went and stood," Romana was within him, that "his soul had a center" (E, 159)—spends the sunny day (in contrast to the purgatorial rains of the day before) around the estate, although he sees Romana only once. Just before his departure in the late afternoon he meets her in the stables, and here again it is the internalized, ideal nature of the relationship that is stressed: "She was as near to him as if she were within him. . . . Everything

[41] The same complex balance of the physical and the metaphysical, of body and soul, is one that Hofmannsthal also stresses repeatedly in his appraisal of the Dante cult of the Pre-Raphaelites in "Über moderne englische Malerei." This quality of moral beauty and spiritualized passion in both Dante and the Pre-Raphaelite painters Hofmannsthal may well have recognized through Pater, who writes (in the chapter from which Hofmannsthal quotes in the essay) that Michelangelo "learns from Dante . . . that for lovers, the surfeiting of desire . . . is a state less happy than poverty with abundance of hope." *The Renaissance* (New York, Modern Library), p. 72.

was taking place outside him and, at the same time, in the very depths of his heart, which until now had never been touched."

Furthermore, after Andreas is on his way back down the darkening valley to the village of Villach, he experiences a vision of Romana that in its vividness and sublimity surpasses all previous visions. Spying above him an eagle whose wings are caught in the last long rays of the late afternoon sun, he is overwhelmed by a transport of the soul in which it is revealed to him that the entire landscape is but the extension of his own inner self. To use William James's description of the religious regeneration of the sick soul, there occurs in Andreas' eyes a "transfiguration of nature. . . . A new heaven seems to shine upon a new earth."[42] In Hofmannsthal's words, he "was aware of nature as never before. It was as if the whole scene had suddenly risen from within him." Borne aloft with the eagle, his spirit senses that, "seen from high enough, the parted are united, and loneliness is an illusion." Furthermore, "wherever he was, he possessed Romana—he could draw her into his very self whenever he wanted." And, just as he had seen her in his dream as doe-like upon her paradisal meadow, he now realizes that she lives within him as the doe lives in the cool shade of the mountain on the opposite side of the valley. "She was a living being, a center, and around her a paradise, no less real than that which towered up on the other side of the valley. He looked into himself, and saw Romana bending down and praying; she bent her knees like the doe when it lays itself to rest." The vision closes with the mystic feeling that "circles dissolved in circles. He prayed together with her, and when he looked over, he saw that the mountain was nothing more than his prayer. An unspeakable

[42] James, *Varieties*, p. 148.

sense of security overcame him: it was the happiest moment of his life" (E, 162).

At this point it might be well to take stock of what we have said about Andreas' love for Romana by viewing its relationship to the overall pattern of love in the Bildungsroman; such an effort may aid us in seeing Andreas' future development in its proper perspective. To begin with, the story of love in the Bildungsroman has most often been a tale of transcendence. Not only *Andreas*, with its parallel to *La Vita Nuova*, but the entire German tradition departs radically from the annals of bourgeois love chronicled by the historical novel. Andreas' love for Romana, as Karl Gautschi has pointed out, is thus very similar to that divine form of love portrayed by both Novalis and Hölderlin, as well as by Goethe.[43] This fact emerges most clearly from the imagery surrounding the traditional heroine of the Bildungsroman. From *Wilhelm Meister* on, she has tended, like Beatrice in the *Paradiso*, to become a divine rather than a domestic protectress, a saint rather than a goodly housewife. Indeed, we can actually speak of a tradition of the transfigured heroine in the Bildungsroman—a tradition whose history still remains to be written and yet whose main points I would like to sketch here for purposes of comparison with *Andreas*. For the Beatrician image of love is not as far removed from the idea of Bildung as we might at first imagine.

In *Wilhelm Meister*, for example, the heroine Natalie not only possesses a name that hints at transcendence ("Christchild"), but also displays spiritual qualities similar to those of her saintly aunt, the Beautiful Soul.[44] Furthermore, the first time she appears before Wilhelm (who is lying stricken on the wooded summit of a mountain following an attack by robbers), she is virtually surrounded by a transfiguring

[43] Gautschi, p. 47. [44] Goethe, *Werke*, VII, 517.

light, like a savior or other-worldly redeemer. A "healing" glance from her eyes affects Wilhelm's already assaulted senses so strongly that "all at once it appeared to him as if her head were encircled with rays, and over her features there seemed to spread little by little a shining light." As consciousness finally fades from him, it seems to him as if a saint is disappearing before his eyes. Similarly, later in the novel (much as Andreas envisions Romana as inhabiting the temple of love within him [E, 158]), Wilhelm tells Natalie that the castle where he has finally found her once more is "no house, but a temple, and you are the worthy priestess, the spirit, of it."[45]

The transfigured heroine also makes her appearance in Novalis' *Heinrich von Ofterdingen*. Whereas to Wilhelm it only *seems* as if he is experiencing a *Märchen*,[46] Heinrich actually does—in the proper sense of the word, of course, which to the romantics signalled a *Märchenwelt* of transcendence. At the opening of the novel's second part, the "Erfüllung" (that is to portray the realization of this ideal, higher realm), Heinrich, who is now a pilgrim, is journeying through the mountains near Augsburg. Suddenly hearing a voice from a nearby tree he pauses, and recognizes the voice as that of Mathilde. "You will remain for a time upon earth," it says, and at this moment he is struck by a blinding ray of light, through which he catches a visionary glimpse of a glorious kingdom in front of which Mathilde stands, full of grace and splendor. As the vision fades he discovers that the "heavenly beam had removed from within him all aches and sorrows" and that death now appeared as merely a "higher revelation of life" itself.

In Hölderlin's *Hyperion* the very name of the heroine indicates her lofty role in the novel, for Diotima is of course the name of that priestess of Mantineia in Plato's *Sym-*

posium from whom Socrates professed to have learned the true nature of love. One day, only a few days after he has met Diotima, Hyperion is suddenly overcome by a strange vision. As he is standing with her on a mountain peak, staring out into the infinity of space, it seems to Hyperion all at once that "Diotima's eyes opened wide; and quietly, as a bud unfolds, her lovely face opened to the breezes of the sky and became pure language and soul; and, as if she were beginning her flight towards the clouds, her whole form rose gently, in easy majesty, to full stature, and she scarcely touched the ground with her feet."[47] The vision of this ascension is central to the entire novel, for in the end Diotima, like Dante's Beatrice and Heinrich's Mathilde, will appear, transformed into a heavenly protectress, as Hyperion's spiritual guide. Moreover, the fact that here, as in both *Wilhelm Meister* and *Heinrich von Ofterdingen*, the vision occurs on a mountain is actually very much in keeping with the Biblical Transfiguration, where Christ's "face did shine as the sun, and his raiment was white as the light," up in "an high mountain" (Matt. 17:1-2).

The transfigured heroine is not, however, limited to the transcendent Bildungsroman of the romanticists, but leaves her traces on the female protagonists of later novels as well, even during the period of realism. In *Der grüne Heinrich*, for example, Heinrich's first vision of Dorothea affects him like a "sunrise," and he finds that the memory of her shining eyes has a "transcendent" effect on him.[48] Similarly, even in so "secular" a work as Stifter's *Nachsommer*, Heinrich Drendorf experiences a prefiguration of his love for Natalie in his epiphany-like encounter with the Greek statue at the Rosenhaus. Not only is the statue, on this particular day,

[47] I, 2 (fifth letter).
[48] Gottfried Keller, *Der grüne Heinrich* in *Sämtliche Werke und ausgewählte Briefe* (Munich, 1963), I, 957-958.

caught in the transfiguring light of a summer evening's thunderstorm, but both Natalie and the marble figure itself are repeatedly described in the novel as symbolically recalling the goddess-like Princess Nausicaa in the *Odyssey*.[49] Much like Goethe's Natalie, who in spite of her Christian qualities and Christian name is referred to throughout the novel as a lovely "Amazon," Stifter's Natalie also combines the features of beautiful saint and pagan princess.[50]

This transcendent quality in the heroine of the German Bildungsroman,[51] her trace of supernal beauty, not only affects her own role in the novel (the transfigured lover, in shedding her bourgeois garb, becoming in part a *divine* bride), but also lends the symbolic background of the *Bildungsreise* a much deeper significance. As we noted in the Introduction, the journey to marriage, profession, and cultural indentures also represents, in varying degrees, a form of *spiritual* pilgrimage. If, moreover, this pilgrimage or quest is to be crowned with the happiness of a more or less ideal love, then we can easily see that Bildung itself is in part at least a transcendent concept. Yet we must hasten to add that there exist two rather different modes of this tran-

[49] Adalbert Stifter, *Der Nachsommer* in *Gesammelte Werke* (Gütersloh, 1956), IV, 334, 616.

[50] It is highly likely that Stifter as well as Goethe was still viewing beauty in this connection through the eyes of Winckelmann, who had expressly suggested that the heads of Greek Amazons be used as models for statues and paintings of the Virgin.

[51] I have profited in this connection from Ludwig Kahn's insights in his *Literatur und Glaubenskrise* (Stuttgart, 1964). Kahn, who views the demise of orthodox belief as preparing for the rise of various meta-religions such as those of Art or Love, notes with specific reference to the "transfigured" Natalie in *Wilhelm Meister*, "Diese Liebe ist nicht Kontrast zum Christentum, sondern wird erst möglich als Ausfluss des Christentums, als transformiertes und sublimiertes Christentum. Liebe als etwas Numinöses, als ein Wunder, als ein den Alltag Transzendierendes . . . ist . . . nachchristliche Religion" (p. 180).

scendence in the Bildungsroman, one that is paradoxically rooted in reality, and another that exists above and beyond the immanent world. *Wilhelm Meister* would be a good example of the first; *Heinrich von Ofterdingen* of the second. For whereas the transcendent aspects of Natalie are firmly anchored in a this-worldly framework of events, the transcendence of Mathilde, like that of the Christian saint or, for that matter, of Dante's Beatrice, is an absolute one. The latter fact is precisely the reason why Mathilde's *death* (and assumption) is so necessary to the eventual "Erfüllung" of the journey; Beatrice's *death* similarly lies at the heart of Dante's new *life*. We might, in fact, distinguish at this point between the two major types of transcendence in the Bildungsroman (its absolute form in Novalis and Hölderlin; its this-worldly form in Goethe, Stifter, and Keller) merely by the simple fact of whether or not the heroine eventually dies.

When we arrive at Hofmannsthal, the obvious dilemma is whether or not the ideal love portrayed in the novel is to be immanent or totally transcendent. From the notes, where this struggle in Hofmannsthal's mind is most evident, it would seem that the former is by far the more likely of the two: that Andreas, in other words, although he is in all likelihood not destined to marry Romana and return with her to Vienna, will indeed come to appreciate her eventually as a love that will enhance his vision and his experience of the world—of this world and not that which comes after. (The *immanent* transcendence involved in this concept of ideal love, as we shall see in the last chapter, was actually to be portrayed much more successfully by Hofmannsthal in his opera libretti, where the written word was to be supported by music.) Andreas, in short, must learn to transform his instinctual love, with all of its frustrations, into a form of ideal devotion. Thus we read in the notes that Andreas,

153

during his stay in Venice, will recall his Romana experience again and again, remembering in detail his walk to the churchyard with her (E, 227), the moment of his sublime vision on the day of his departure (E, 197), and other similar events. Gradually he is to become aware of how "one moment can contain within it an entire lifetime" (E, 223), how, as Sacramozo echoes, "one must be of a genius-like nature (like Francis of Assisi) to be determined forever by a single experience" (E, 203). Just as anything can furnish "substance for the divine" (E, 202), so Andreas experiences a "constant sublimation of the substance Romana through everything that happens: he can only possess Romana when he *has faith* in her" (E, 226). He thus senses "how Romana begins to exist within him: single features, a smile, as if in understanding with him" (E, 227) and eventually, after many such recollections, he feels himself actually "wedded" to her (E, 224).

On the other hand, it must be admitted, however, that there are occasional comments in the notes that hint at the development of a totally transcendent love, much like that portrayed by Dante. Thus at one point Andreas, in a terrifying vision, imagines that he has murdered Romana and "in his mind he pictures to himself all that he has destroyed in Romana; he does not allow her to die completely, but to go on living as a joyless spirit—only then does he become aware of the richness of her life; he feels at one with her as never before, he suddenly perceives the meaning of life—he is blissfully happy" (E, 226). Furthermore, he is desperately jealous of Sacramozo's totally Platonic relationship—his " 'intransitive' friendship"—with Maria (E, 213), and within him there arises together with his desire for possession the equally "deep impulse toward non-possession" (E, 238). His most intense experience of all, in fact, is the "sensation in himself of all love *and* no love" (E, 226; my italics). Yet in spite of these traces of a total transcendence, we must guard against making the parallel with Dante absolute and thus turning Romana into a shadowy, spiritual mediatress with the divine. For in Andreas' character there is mirrored, in a sense, that same love-hate affair with transcendence that Hofmannsthal himself had experienced in his early encounters with Neoplatonic recollection. Andreas may indeed come to realize his love for Romana more fully through Sacramozo (E, 203), who is a Neoplatonist,[51a] but he will most likely not raise her to the Neoplatonist's level of a totally abstract love. Hofmannsthal himself was too well aware of the folly of truly Platonic love to have intended to portray this in his novel; just two years before he began *Andreas*, in fact, he entered in his journal the following note, which, although it refers to the figure of Semiramis, could also be read as a perfect parody of the Platonic lover: "A man murders one lover after another, because she stands between him and Love" (A, 142).

Confronting Andreas, then, when he arrives in Venice, is a twofold task: he must, on the one hand, learn to accept the shameful experiences with Gotthilff as a necessary part of reality and, on the other, he must begin to understand his love for Romana in a sense that would make of her a form of ideal, and thus deepen his sense of life in general. The two acts are integrally related, for the former would assert the necessity of suffering and guilt in life, the inescapable reality of past experience, whereas the latter, operating through imagination as well as memory, would affirm future time as well, thus putting Andreas in a sense *beyond* the reach of ordinary time. This he will learn, in fact, in conversations with Sacramozo, who indicates to him that one

---

[51a] See *Hugo von Hofmannsthal, Erzählungen und Aufsätze*, ed. Rudolf Hirsch (Frankfurt a. M., 1961), p. 163. The "Platonismus" mentioned in the first edition (E, 234) has been amended in the later one to read "Platonismus des Maltesers."

must learn to affirm, "from one's present standpoint, the chain of experiences as necessary" (E, 244) and, further-more, that the course of the future depends directly upon this interpretation of the past. "If I," Andreas muses, "was just anyone when she first kissed me, then everything is meaningless; if I was the only one (with the anticipation of all time until death), then it is sublime. Love is the antici-pation of the end in the beginning and is therefore victory over transience, over time, even over death" (E, 243). In spite of the intimations of transcendence here, however (Hofmannsthal also mentions Novalis), Romana most likely would have become an ideal for Andreas in a world lying *this side* of the Christian world of transcendence. The "heaven" Andreas may eventually find in her (E, 247) will in all probability be neither that of Dante nor that of Novalis, but rather that of Rilke and other modern writers for whom heaven is, peculiarly, a phenomenon of this-worldliness.[52] Andreas' love for Romana, together with its necessary complement of self-love, his accession to whole-ness,[53] must take place in a world of *inner* transcendence.

[52] The question of the difference between Dante's world-view and that of Hofmannsthal, one which involves the problem of an increasingly secularized, subjective idealism, is far more complex than I have indicated here, for it inhabits that difficult ground be-tween metaphysics and psychology. For a deeper discussion of this problem, as reflected in literature, see Erich Kahler's article, "Die Verinnerung des Erzählens," *Neue Rundschau*, 68 (1957), 501-547. What I designate as an immanent transcendence in Andreas' love for Romana would be a variant of what Kahler terms an "aufsteigende Symbolik."

[53] Cf. his "higher egocentricity" (E, 244), and the fact that this "enjoyment of the self" is possible only through Romana (E, 196).

NINE   The Mythic Substructure:

Three Images

Dass für ihn der Reichtum des sittlich Möglichen in
Gestalten, nicht in Begriffen sich innerlich darstelle, da-
durch unterscheidet sich, der den Tempel der Bildung
betreten hat, von dem im Vorhof Verweilenden.

(A, 48-49)

In 1917, ten years after he had begun work on
Andreas, Hofmannsthal received a letter from his
friend Rudolf Pannwitz in which Pannwitz mentions certain Alpine myths that exist in the Ladin language (a
Rhaeto-Romanic dialect spoken in the Engadine, Switzerland, and in adjacent parts of the Austro-Italian
Alps). Hofmannsthal's reaction to this chance information is highly interesting with regard to the flashback
section of *Andreas*. "The Ladin myths," he writes, "—
where are they available?—this is very important to me
for many reasons; because it belongs to the Austrian
world, and because precisely this layer is missing in my
novel, whose first part [describes] a trip of the hero to
Venice, with a certain adventure in the Tirolean-Carin-
thian area on the border of the Ladin region, and I have
continually sought within me for a deeper, more mysterious layer that could come into play, but have found nothing; [I] knew nothing of these Ladin sagas."[54]

Although he may not have been aware of these particular myths when he began writing *Andreas*, Hofmannsthal actually did provide the novel with that

[54] "Aus Hofmannsthals Briefen an Rudolf Pannwitz," *Mesa*,
5 (1955), 28.

"deeper, more mysterious layer" he refers to in the letter. Existing less on the level of theme than on that of image, this "mythic" layer or pattern in the novel actually represents a phenomenon that occurs often in Hofmannsthal's writings. The poet was extremely fond of concealing his deepest ideas, as he put it, on the surface of his prose,[55] of introducing the most complex themes on the levels of style, syntax, imagery, and character-configuration. Indeed, it is this aspect of Hofmannsthal that most fascinates and at the same time most perplexes: the themes are straightforward, and yet the imagistic fabric in which they are presented is so complex that the obvious becomes infinitely elusive. It is this infinite quality of the imagistic surface of the novel that we shall investigate here and that, to employ Hofmannsthal's own definition of the term, I have called "mythic." To begin with, however, both because of a devaluation of this term through its overuse in modern criticism, and because there exists, to my knowledge, no study of Hofmannsthal's own conception of myth,[56] it will first be necessary to give a short résumé of Hofmannsthal's understanding of the term.

Nowhere in his works does Hofmannsthal set forth a

[55] Cf. "Die Tiefe muss man verstecken. Wo? An der Oberfläche" (A, 47), and: "Die bedeutenden Deutschen scheinen immer unter Wasser zu schwimmen, nur Goethe, wie ein einsamer Delphin, streicht auf der spiegelnden Oberfläche" (A, 80).

[56] Kobel, who treats myth in connection with both *Der Turm* and *Die ägyptische Helena*, nowhere gives a clear exposition of what Hofmannsthal precisely understood by the term, employing it rather in a general way to support his chief theme of the "Antinomie von Sein und Werden" (*Hugo von Hofmannsthal* [Berlin, 1970], p. 235; see also pp. 218-219, 331-335, 346-348). Rolf Tarot, *Hugo von Hofmannsthal: Daseinsformen und dichterische Struktur* (Tübingen, 1970), who employs "mythic consciousness" to interpret Hofmannsthal's *early* works, merely equates the term with pre-existence (p. 173).

specific aesthetic, and to determine his particular understanding of "myth" (like that of the related term "symbol"),
we must first synthesize a definition from his various writings, particularly from the notebooks and the essays. Myth
for Hofmannsthal is first of all a form of believed fiction,
something that is either remembered or imagined and yet
that we experience with the intensity of a lived event. This
much, at least, he tells us in his *Buch der Freunde*: "Everything imaginary, in which you truly participate, is mythical"
(A, 34-35).[57] There must, in other words, be a personal
commitment to the fiction. As Hofmannsthal notes elsewhere, a myth therefore usually develops in the context of
the "actions and sufferings of individuals" (A, 233). Second,
the symbolic import of myth must assume the form of a
coincidentia oppositorum, a dynamic balance of opposites.
"In myth everything has a double and counter meaning:
death = life, snake-fight = love-embrace. Hence in myth
everything is balanced" (A, 35)—an idea that connects
Hofmannsthal's thought with much of mythic thinking in
general.[58] Third, this oxymoronic structure of meaning in
myth is usually supported by a similar pattern in the
imagery; appropriating a phrase suggested by the visual
arts, Hofmannsthal speaks of a form of imagistic chiaroscuro, a quality of *Helldunkel*, that underlies most myths.
Last of all, he hints at a mysterious process of "crystallization" that must take place in the mind of the individual
whenever a new myth is born. "The formation of myths is
like the crystallization of a saturated solution: in the decisive moment everything becomes mythical, just like the

[57] "Mythisch ist alles Erdichtete, woran du als Lebender Anteil
hast."

[58] Mircea Eliade, in his *Patterns in Comparative Religion*, trans.
R. Sheed (Cleveland, 1966), speaks specifically of the "mythical
pattern" as being one of a "coincidentia oppositorum" (p. 419 f.)

159

little dog at the feet of the knight" (A, 233).[59] The last example, as we shall see, actually contains an oblique reference to *Andreas*.

That a myth is usually grounded in an imagery of chiaroscuro emerges from Hofmannsthal's lecture, "Shakespeares Könige und grosse Herren" (a study that in turn forms an interesting counterpart to Heine's "Shakespeares Mädchen und Frauen" as well as to Pater's "Shakespeare's English Kings").[60] Proceeding as usual by a method of indirection, Hofmannsthal argues that myth, designated here simply as Homeric myth, displays the same structural characteristics as do certain works in painting and drama. Selecting Rem-

[59] In general, of course, an "individual" myth would represent a contradiction in terms. What is mythical is typical, and precisely not limited to the experience of one individual. Yet in Hofmannsthal's usage this is possible, for he would include in the term the idea of the *Urerlebnis*, the experience of the individual that becomes in later years so deeply formative that it represents a truly "primal" or "archetypal" experience. In this sense, Dante's experience with Beatrice ultimately became a mythical one and Andreas' encounter with Romana may eventually do the same. It might be added that Hofmannsthal's concept of myth, concentrating as it does on the structure of experience rather than its content, could also be applied to other works of his as well—works that feature similar orchestrations of opposites supported by an imagery of chiaroscuro. It is a pattern that repeats itself in his works again and again, from "Manche freilich" to *Der Turm*, and is even found in the starkly dualistic Greek plays of the middle period. As he himself states in later years, "Auch dort wo Kontraste dargestellt sind, in der mittleren Periode, wie die heroische Elektra und die nur weibliche Chrysothemis, oder der starke Pierre und der schwache Jaffier, kam es mir immer darauf an, dass sie mitsammen eine Einheit bildeten, recht eigentliche *eins* waren" (A, 234).

[60] Appearing in *Appreciations* (London, 1931), Pater's essay, together with the essays in the same volume on *Love's Labour's Lost* and *Measure for Measure*, actually foreshadows to a surprising degree Hofmannsthal's own insights into Shakespeare, namely, that the plays present (1) studies in contrasts, constructions in light and shade, and (2) pictorial configurations, groups set against a common background, as against a tapestry (pp. 169, 180, 186, 193).

brandt and Shakespeare as examples, he focuses on what he sees as the central quality of their work, one he terms a dynamic interplay of opposites. Thus in Rembrandt's paintings, it is the *Helldunkel* that fascinates him, for he sees in them an interdependence of surface and depth, of bright figures and dark background. Standing before a Rembrandt, he notes, we are unable to say "whether the atmosphere is there for the sake of the figures, or the figures for the sake of the atmosphere" (PII, 145). Figure and ground, in terms of the total pattern or *Gestalt*, are inseparable. In Shakespeare, the dynamic configurations—ensembles, Hofmannsthal calls them—are much the same: they represent Rembrandts sprung to life, as it were. The "illusion" of depth has become on the stage a reality, and yet there still prevails the same interdependence of figure and ground; the static figure has merely been transformed into a dramatic character, the aesthetic pattern into an ethical one in its broadest sense. For just as there is in Rembrandt a mystical dependence of white upon black, black upon white, so in Shakespeare there is a contingency of character on environment and environment on character. Each character fulfills himself and yet in so doing somehow participates in the total ensemble as well. There thus arises, in Hofmannsthal's eyes, a unity of all of the players with all of the space that mystically surrounds and connects them with one another.[61]

When we turn to *Andreas* with these ideas in mind, the mythic pattern informing both the episodes and the imagery springs into view immediately. Everywhere there are mythic blacks and whites, particularly in the counter-

[61] Michael Hamburger sees in this concept of a mystic "space between characters" an early formulation by Hofmannsthal of that concept he later termed the "allomatic." See Hamburger's "Introduction" to the *Selected Plays and Libretti* of Hofmannsthal (New York, 1963), p. xx.

point that links Gotthilff and Romana. Romana, for instance, is constantly depicted in tones of brightness and light: during the noon meal she "lights up" with joy at every breath (E, 131); in the churchyard she looks over the graves with "radiant brown eyes" (E, 134); that evening her dark eyes "flash at every word" (E, 137); and in Andreas' dream that night, her eyes again are "shining" in a strange manner (E, 157-158). Gotthilff, on the other hand, belongs to the realms of darkness. It is already late at night when Andreas first encounters him in the inn at Villach and the next day Gotthilff returns "before it was fully light" (E, 125). At the Finazzerhof Gotthilff spends the entire afternoon in the gloom of the stables, and the following morning has made his getaway before darkness has lifted.

Yet beyond this simple polar pattern there exists an even closer counterpoint, one which actually maps the interaction of the extremes in the mind and memory of Andreas. He and Gotthilff, for example, arrive at the Finazzerhof under the foreboding sign of a black sky pierced by only occasional flashes of sunshine, and the first afternoon's episodes similarly alternate between the bright scenes with Romana and the dark stable scenes with Gotthilff. That same evening the clash—now centered in Andreas' own consciousness—becomes even more evident: "At supper a feeling he had never known overcame Andreas: everything was in pieces: the darkness and the light" (E, 141); later he overhears Romana's parents talking of a couple with "white hair . . . like silver" who had drowned in the *Schwarz*bach (E, 142). When he arrives at Romana's door, "everything stood out clearly in black and white" (E, 143), and it is the presence in the room of the maid with "white-streaked hair" amid the "dark shadows" that then drives Andreas back to his own room to brood and look out upon the dark courtyard lit by the strange brightness of the full moon (where he catches sight of the dog who, unknown to him, is dying from the poison given him by Gotthilff). Several hours later, the chiaroscuro of events culminates in the night-time fire.

The *Helldunkel* does not end, however, with Gotthilff's flight. Following the interim period of a day, in which a weather of grey cloudiness predominates, the vivid contrasts return once more—this time, however, in harmonious balance with one another, as if, in Hofmannsthal's sense of the mythical, both the darkness and the light were dependent upon one another. The day opens with Andreas' prophetic dream of Romana in her earthly paradise, where everything is at once "darkest and most radiant" (E, 157). The day closes with the scene of Andreas' taking leave of Romana in the dark interior of the stables: at Romana's entrance, there is a sudden burst of sunlight through a small window and the scene is bathed in light. And finally, as Andreas departs from the Finazzerhof the entire mountain landscape assumes the chiaroscuro tones of a mythical painting: as the long shadows reach out from the foot of the mountains into the valleys, the late afternoon sun catches the tallest peaks in a final fiery brilliance; and for a moment at least, the entire world assumes for Andreas that magical *Helldunkel* that Hofmannsthal understood as the underlying principle of the mythic pattern.

Yet we have investigated only one aspect of myth as Hofmannsthal saw it. A second condition is that it present, on a level of meaning more articulate than that of mere chiaroscuro, a form of *coincidentia oppositorum*. This aspect of the novel, though not so obvious as that of the symbolic shading, is fully as important. Three images in particular in the flashback section suggest this mythic equation of a unity within a polarity. They are the images of the horse, the bird, and the dog, symbolizing respectively the realms of the sensual, the spiritual, and their mythical coincidence. The imagery of the horse and stable, undoubtedly the most obvious of the three, connects throughout the flashback with the forbidden realms of sex, guilt, and erotic desire—realms most generally associated with Gotthilff. The servant first lures Andreas into accepting him as a traveling companion by displaying the "spirited little horse" to him in the courtyard beneath his window (E, 125). In similar fashion, on the first afternoon of their journey, Gotthilff accidentally spurs his horse against Andreas' precisely at a moment when he is describing his nightly enjoyment of a local woman some years earlier: "It had been well worth while. She had had black hair, right down to the back of her knees. At that he spurred on his little horse and rode right up to Andreas, so that Andreas had to warn him to take care" (E, 126-127). And again, when Gotthilff adds the comment that the ladies of the region are freer with their charms than are the peasant girls, he rides up so close to Andreas that Andreas is physically repelled (E, 128).

Soon, however, his blood heated by the servant's stories, Andreas himself begins to be caught up in sexual fantasies, and imagines that he, who "had never seen, let alone touched, a naked woman" (E, 126), is seducing a countess. Suddenly, however, he sees the servant beside him in the dream, "emptying his gun on a woman who had crept up to him in her nightdress" (E, 129) and at this, as a violent reaction to these carnal fantasies, Andreas unconsciously reins in his horse, causing Gotthilff's horse to stumble and injure its leg. The next day, after they have been forced to put in at the Finazzer farm, Gotthilff, as we have already mentioned, spends most of the day in the stables, preparing the saltpeter that would "make a sick horse sound and a sound dog sick" (E, 138). As a final touch, after he has actually fled the farm before daylight the next morning—on

Andreas' horse—the servant girl Gotthilff had assaulted is wrapped in a horse-blanket. We do not need to have read Freud or Jung to decipher the meaning of the horse symbol here. In each case it is associated directly in Andreas' mind with a vision of carnal love. From the phallic image of the gun to the more subtle image of the horse-blanket, the surface texture of the episode reflects the major theme: Andreas' inability to come to terms with the dark side of love, with his own unconscious erotic desire.[62]

With our second image, that of the bird, whose symbolic connotations are the opposite of those of the horse, the pattern is perhaps not so immediately obvious. In general, the bird represents the realm of the spirit, and thus of Romana and the world of light. A high point of the first afternoon, for instance, comes when Romana, after showing Andreas a heraldic eagle in a book of hers, takes him to the top of one of the four towers marking the boundary of the estate and shows him the family mascot: an eagle originally captured by her grandfather; as they enter, a flash of light seems to cross its aged face. Yet it is not until the third day that the bird image assumes its greatest importance when it appears at three strategic points in the story, each of them relating directly to Andreas' love for Romana. The first of these we have already discussed: it is Andreas' prophetic discovery of the bird on his windowsill. The second, fully as important, takes place in the stables when Andreas takes leave of Romana: as she enters the barn, a swallow darts through a shaft of sunlight—a touch that, like the image of the horse, is entirely realistic and yet at the same time deeply symbolic. Indeed, the moment is portrayed with

[62] It would be interesting to compare Hofmannsthal's use of the horse symbol here with its use in the *Reitergeschichte*, the *672. Märchen*, and in *Bassompierre*, where it also plays a prominent role. See also the last line of the poem "Vor Tag."

such quick, impressionistic strokes that it is almost as if everything were a dream in Andreas' mind, for before he knows it he is alone once more. Yet the symbolic conjunction of sunlight and darkness, of the bird and the stable, gives us the first hint that Andreas' love for Romana may have begun to accept and transcend its darker, unconscious side. The final appearance of the bird symbol occurs at Andreas' departure,[63] which takes place only minutes after he leaves Romana: in a supremely symbolic scene, an eagle, soaring high above the "mythic" conjunction of sunlight and darkness, becomes the focus of Andreas' realization that all things, when viewed from high enough, are united.

The last of our three images—that of the dog—is at the same time the most allusively employed and the most important. For in this one symbol the polarities represented by the bird and the horse in Andreas' unconscious are both synthesized and transcended. Spirit and sense, innocence and guilt, light and darkness all converge in this one image and form that all-embracing reality that Hofmannsthal calls "mythic," and that William James, referring to the healing process of the sick soul, terms the "deepest levels of truth."[64] On the one hand, the dog is obviously associated with Gotthilff's world, with the stable and the horses, for the Finaz-

[63] Although birds also appear in the Venetian episodes—Zustina and Nina have pet birds in cages, Andreas' sudden vision of Mariquita through a grape trellis in Nina's courtyard is accompanied by the violent reactions of a bird in a nearby cage, and Sacramozo poses the mystic question, "How . . . can a chameleon change into an eagle?" (E, 237)—the image of the *caged* bird here seems to suggest that Andreas' deeper spiritual self still awaits liberation. The bird as symbol of the spirit also occurs elsewhere in Hofmannsthal, as in the image of the crucified sparrow-hawk at the beginning of "Dämmerung und nächtliches Gewitter"; and the idea of birds in flight as "dimly sensed world-forces" is one active in his poetry (G, 496) as well as in his essay "Die Wege und die Begegnungen."

[64] James, *Varieties*, p. 160.

zer dog is poisoned by Gotthilff with the brew prepared in the stable as a cure for the horse. On the other hand, Andreas naturally associates the dog with Romana and the Finazzers, not only because it figures as a family pet but also because it appears in the family's heraldic sign. When he is on his afternoon walk to the village churchyard with Romana he notices a large reddish tombstone set into the church wall behind the Finazzer graves; on it is carved "the figure of a knight, fully armed, with his helmet on his arm, [and] at his feet was a little dog, so lifelike that he merely seemed to be sleeping there, his paws resting on the coat of arms" (E, 134). The dog image not only plays a role within the story, however, but also connects with one of the general statements on myth in Hofmannsthal's notebooks. For in *Ad me ipsum* he remarks (and this was our last criterion for myth) that the "formation of myths is like the crystallization of a saturated salt solution: in the decisive moment everything becomes mythical, just like the little dog at the feet of the knight" (E, 233). In retrospect, in other words— through Andreas' memory—the dog can become part of a particular mythic pattern.

Yet the note, like so many in *Ad me ipsum*, is not entirely clear. What does Hofmannsthal mean, for instance, by "crystallization"? And how does this connect with a process involving memory and imagination? One possible answer is suggested by the fact that we know, through Hamburger's report on Hofmannsthal's library, that Hofmannsthal possessed a copy of Stendhal's study of romantic love, *De l'Amour* (Paris, 1896), and that he read this while he was working on his Venetian comedy *Cristinas Heimreise*[65] (ca. 1907)—a period that also saw the first draft of *Andreas*. For "crystallization" is one of the leading metaphors with which Stendhal attempts to explain the psychological

---

[65] Hamburger, "Hofmannsthals Bibliothek," p. 48.

transformations that take place when one falls in love. Using as an analogy the practice of Salzburg salt-miners of leaving dead branches in the mines until they collect a covering of glittering, diamond-like crystals, he speaks of the phenomenon that we know of today as psychological projection. The lover beginning to love, he states, proceeds to clothe his beloved in just such a crystalline beauty. Through memory and imagination, in other words, the lover deifies his beloved to such an extent that his image of her would be totally unrecognizable to anyone else.[66] With very little effort, we can see how Hofmannsthal might well have viewed this process of "crystallization" as the equivalent of constructing a private myth. (Stendhal's comment that for the Austrian woman love is virtually a "religion" would certainly have appealed to Hofmannsthal as well.)[67]

The note in *Ad me ipsum* is not the only indication that Andreas' love for Romana may eventually attain a mythic dimension. Another book Hofmannsthal was reading in connection with the novel, several years later, contains several jottings referring to *Andreas*, two of which are directly relevant to our findings here. The title of the book alone, *Probleme der Mystik und ihrer Symbolik*,[68] indicates Hofmannsthal's general interests at the time. The two notes are as follows: "The constant sublimation [*Erhöhung*] of the substance Romana (= reality) through everything that happens; he can only possess Romana when he has faith in her," and: "mythical = that in which you, as a living person, bodily participate. In myth everything exists through its double meaning."[69] This last definition, as we have noted,

---

[66] Stendhal, *On Love*, trans. H.B.V. (New York, 1967), in particular pp. 28-35 and 362-365.

[67] *Ibid.*, p. 181.

[68] Herbert Silberer (n.p., 1914); this work greatly influenced Hofmannsthal's later notes to *Andreas*, particularly with regard to the figure of Sacramozo. See T. Wieser, "Der Malteser," pp. 24-29.

[69] Quoted in Alewyn, *Über Hugo von Hofmannsthal*, p. 160.

was to pass, practically unaltered, into the *Buch der Freunde* (A, 34-35). More important, however, is the fact that the two notes occur next to one another in precisely the same context, for this, in addition to our investigation of imagery, indicates that the idea of myth was closely connected in Hofmannsthal's mind with both the figure of Romana and the problem of ideal love. Moreover, the notion of an elevated love actually appeared in the notes for the novel at two different points: once almost literally (E, 226), and again in a more general sense (interestingly enough, directly following a quotation from Silberer concerning the alchemical healing of the inner self): "In love: always sublimate, volatilize, sacrifice life, the moment, for the higher, more pure thing that is to be produced—seek to fix this that is higher, more pure" (E, 237).

To return to the image of the dog, we can now perhaps appreciate more fully the fact that this emblem somehow becomes associated with the deeper reality Andreas experiences through his encounters with both Gotthilff and Romana. The dog comes to function as a symbol of the mythical conjunction of extremes. It is not merely fortuitous that the image of the horse occurs most frequently on the first day, that of the bird on the third, and Andreas' vision of mythic unity, of a world beyond, on the second—at the grave of the Finazzer dog. And in this vision, much as in his dream the same night, his being seems to merge with that of Gotthilff, just as the dog beneath the earth merges in his mind with his memory of the dog he had had as a boy, which he had killed in a moment of brutish cruelty.

The fact that this epiphany occurs because of certain memories connected with an animal is not as unlikely as it might at first appear, particularly when we recall Hofmannsthal's own attitude toward such matters. Like Rilke, he was extraordinarily sensitive to the presence of animals. The tale of his abrupt exit from a Viennese café when

169

Stefan George swore and kicked at a dog is well known[70] (for several years afterwards, Hofmannsthal refused even to see George), and from the "Terzinen" we know that dogs in general possessed for him a being "unheimlich stumm und fremd," like some strange alter ego. In a diary note on the *Nibelungenlied*, for instance, Hofmannsthal reminds us of the fact that Siegfried's dog, following his master's murder, also dies (A, 158). Moreover, because of this mystical kinship with human beings, animals, in Hofmannsthal's eyes, could also die a sacrificial death for human beings, functioning in a sense as redeemers. In a poem of 1894 about a dog drowned in Lake Como, for example, he passes from a description of the animal's sad death to the mystical assertion, in the final line, of the "Einigkeit von alledem im Sein" (BI, 116). Similarly, in the second part of the "Augenblicke in Griechenland," the Greek epigraph to the effect that "Even dogs suffer from the Erinyes" would also seem to associate dogs with the ideas of suffering and redemption (the Erinyes serving as both Furies *and* Eumenides).[71]

Moreover, in "Der Dichter und diese Zeit," written the same year that *Andreas* was begun, Hofmannsthal mentions that as a child he would often spend hours on end imagining in a most horrifying manner the "torment of animals, of mistreated horses, caged creatures"; once he even imagined a "wild-animal tamer who kills his lions by throwing poisoned meat to them. It happened in a sphere of dark, strong, child-like feeling, this imagining, [and] it was not as clear as these words present it; it was nothing but a hollow pain and the sympathetic, half-horrifying imagining of a situation in which torment was mixed with *redemption*. . . .

[70] George-Hofmannsthal *Briefwechsel*, ed. R. Boehringer (Munich, 1953), p. 236.

[71] Kobel points out (p. 189) that in Greek drama a similar identification exists: the Furies (or Eumenides) were often compared to or even represented as dogs.

Thousands of children," he concludes, "experience more pain from the suffering of animals than they ever let on" (PII, 379; my italics).[71a] Elsewhere he reports that as a youth he had often immersed himself in "false and imagined pain" in order to experience "something infinite" (PIII, 170), that he had "delighted in his own pain" in order to "expand the scale of his sensibility" (PI, 132). In *Lucidor*, Vladimir similarly recalls his childhood ability to empathize in a deeply sensuous manner "with an animal, a dog," or even "a swan" (E, 106), and in the *Frau ohne Schatten* the Emperor's aim during the hunt is suddenly rendered unsteady by the strange glance from the eye of the cornered gazelle (E, 258).

The parallels here to the redemptive role of the poisoned Finazzer dog and to the feeling of infinity that sweeps over Andreas at the memory of the dying glance of his own dog, as well as at that of the cat he had killed, are obvious. Indeed, the strange closeness of animals to human beings, their ability to die redemptive, sacrificial deaths, was an idea so real to Hofmannsthal that he could actually employ it as a metaphor to explain the process of mystical identification in general. In "Das Gespräch über Gedichte," for instance, he equates the symbolism of poetry with the symbolism of animal sacrifice. The magical connection between image and reader is the same, he states, as that between totem and believer (the swan image mentioned above recurs here as well). For the world, in the eyes of the poet or the priest, is a mystic whole, and in true poetry, much as in the liturgy, allegory does not exist; transubstantiation—mystical identification—is all (PII, 87-90).[72]

[71a] The "Danish story" Hofmannsthal mentions in this same context is "Fratelli Bedini" by Herman Bang.

[72] The deeply monistic and ultimately romantic world-view propounded in this discourse on the literary symbol is also present in later discussions of the subject by Hofmannsthal. Yet because the

The dog, then, to return to the novel, functions in Andreas' mind as a sort of mythic emblem, merging in his thoughts with the memories of horses and birds and connecting with that "world beyond the real world" (E, 156) envisioned at the dog's grave. This is suggested not only by our interpretations here, but also by a comment of one of Hofmannsthal's close friends. Rudolf Kassner, in remarking that Hofmannsthal, far more than Rilke even, experienced his deepest, most personal moments in a form of mystical dream-state, relates how Hofmannsthal had once explained to him that this realm of deepest experience he termed "Welt hinter der Welt"; this world beyond ordinary reality, Kassner explains, is what we normally call "Mythos."[73] In mythical thought, according to Hofmannsthal, light finds its foundation in darkness (the *Helldunkel* pattern), Eros in Thanatos (the love-embrace and the snake-fight), and so on, much in the same way that evil, for James's sick soul, "must have its foundation in God."[74] Just as the world of the

formulation becomes progressively more abstract (a characteristic of Hofmannsthal's late style in general), the notion of the symbol actually tends to merge with that of myth, for both of course center upon a sort of *unio mystica*. Thus Hofmannsthal comments in a late essay that Greek *symbola* actually means "Zusammenwerfung des Unvereinbaren" (PIII, 479) and, in another essay, that "Mythenbildung" is none other than the formation of the symbol, which in turn is merely "das sinnliche Bild für geistige Wahrheit, die der ratio unerreichbar ist" (PIV, 49). From these metaphors alone, it is clear that the mystical center of existence had shifted for Hofmannsthal from the temple of the body to that of the spirit.

[73] Rudolf Kassner, "Erinnerung an Hugo v. Hofmannsthal," in *Hugo von Hofmannsthal: Der Dichter im Spiegel der Freunde*, ed. H. Fiechtner (Bern, 1963), pp. 249-250.

[74] James, *Varieties*, p. 129; here again we are reminded of the epiphany of another modern *Bildungsheld*. Hans Castorp, brought face to face with death by an Alpine snowstorm, suddenly perceives that "Man is the lord of counter-positions"—mythical ones, we might

sick soul is "vastly more complex" and his sense of life a much "deeper kind of conscious being,"[75] so Andreas' mythical world is "not as empty, as desolate, as this one" (E, 156). The world of myth, although James does not use this word specifically, is the world into which the sick soul must be reborn, and it is the one that Andreas must begin to form in his own mind, centering on the mythical images of the dog, the bird, and the horse.

These images, however, belong more to Andreas' subconscious than to his conscious mind; and the same could be said for the reader of the novel as well. For although we have "allegorized" them in this section, the three chief images do not represent anything other than themselves; to insist on the contrary would be to devalue them to the status of unreal symbols, to hang real trees, in Hofmannsthal's words, with paper blossoms (PII, 87). Hofmannsthal, as we recall, was fond of concealing his complexity on the surface, and there is perhaps no better example of this than his use of the dog image in the Venetian episodes. Here again the dog symbolizes a conjunction of mythical extremes: for it is the spiritual Maria and the sensuous Mariquita—reflecting the latent split in Andreas' own personality—who possess *between them* the "tiny, short-winded King Charles spaniel by the name of Fidèle" (E, 207).[76]

---

add—and that civilization can only exist "in silent recognition of the blood-sacrifice." *The Magic Mountain*, trans. H. T. Lowe-Porter (New York, Modern Library), p. 496.

[75] James, *Varieties*, p. 154.

[76] Maria's Fidèle is, of course, the little dog referred to in the title of an earlier draft of the novel, "Die Dame mit dem Hündchen." Whether or not Hofmannsthal was influenced in this motif and title by Chekhov's "The Lady with the Pet Dog," a short story featuring a heroine who, like Maria, is unhappily married and has a strange affair is probably impossible to determine.

Venedig, das traumhafteste und theatralischeste historische
oder architektonische Gebilde, das es auf der Welt gibt. . . .
(A, 338)

HERE ARE all sorts of nooks and corners and hiding-
places; the city is full of private staircases, secret
doors, and clandestine abodes whose mystery not 'jeal-
ousy herself' could spy out. In this maze of canals, this
labyrinth of lanes, you might play a splendid game of
hide-and-seek. And so Venice is the ideal city for adventures, the home for the adventurer." So writes Philippe
Monnier in his book *Venise au dix-huitième Siècle*
(Paris, 1907),[77] in a chapter appropriately entitled "The
Adventurers: Casanova." And in Venice—on the 27th of
June, 1907, at the Lido—Hofmannsthal sat reading these
lines, letting his imagination be stirred for several of the
literary projects he had in mind at the time, among them
Andreas. Leafing through other chapters of the book, he
also came across "The Venetian Theater and Italian
Comedy," a topic that had already fascinated him for
some years, and two paragraphs in particular must have
caught his eye: "The horizon of the Venetians seemed to
be bounded by footlights, stage scenery, and a prompt-

[77] Monnier, p. 190; all quotations and paginations in this section are taken from the English edition: Philippe Monnier,
Venice in the Eighteenth Century (Boston, 1910). According to
Alewyn and Hamburger, Hofmannsthal looked at chapters I, IV,
VIII, IX, and XI in 1907, chapter X in 1908, chapter I again in
1911, chapter XI again in 1913, and chapters IX and X once more
in 1916. Cf. Hamburger's report on Hofmannsthal's library, p. 48,
and Alewyn, *Über Hugo von Hofmannsthal*, p. 129.

174

er's box. . . . Of all this busy hurrying population there was scarcely a person who had not some connection with the stage, as lamp-lighter or ticket-collector, as box-attendant or copyist of music, as chorus girl or her dressmaker. . . . At every corner of this fantastic city there stood out a group of wandering comedians." While a "troupe of opera-singers is waiting on the quay at St. Mosé to embark at break of day," for instance, elsewhere in the city the "mother of a singer is drawing the lottery, which she has organised to meet the needs of her daughter."[78]

Filling his imagination with these and other scenes drawn by Monnier (in a book that reads more like good fiction than history), Hofmannsthal thus prepared to begin the first draft of his novel—three pages with the title, "Venetian Travel-Diary of the Herr von N. (1779)." Indeed, this short draft contains a note for an opening scene in which the hero, arriving at daybreak, finds a "troupe of actors waiting on the beach" as well as another note to the effect that all of the people whom the hero encounters in his new lodgings "are connected with the theater" (E, 192-193). And in the final version of the novel, we encounter the same situation: Andreas' landlady is a box-attendant; her husband is a lamp-lighter; their elder daughter has until recently been an actress (E, 119); and Zorzi, whose room Andreas takes, is a designer and painter of stage scenery. Moreover, the family is also holding a lottery to better themselves financially. And just as Monnier, in describing the city of courtesans and cicisbei in his chapter "Venetian Love," mentions the name Nina in conjunction with the "houris of this paradise of lovers,"[79] so Hofmannsthal names the elder daughter of the family, an actress-courtesan, Nina as well.

Yet why Venice as setting, why a city of fantasy as stage

---

[78] Monnier, pp. 130-132.   [79] Ibid., p. 62.

for a serious Bildungsroman? Goethe, for instance, had set his Bildungsroman on solid German ground, "between the forests of Thuringia and the sandy wastes of Mecklenburg";[80] Novalis had placed the realistic portions of his novel between Eisenach and Augsburg; and Stifter and Keller had set their Bildungsromane in Austria, Switzerland, and Germany. Why, then, did Hofmannsthal choose Venice? First of all, it was because Venice, of all foreign cities, greatly appealed to him, a fact attested to by his repeated visits there throughout his life. In terms of the novel, it was because Venice, practically alone among western European cities, was, in Hofmannsthal's own words, "traumhaft" as well as "historisch." The fact, interestingly enough, issues very clearly from Monnier's book as well. On the one hand it was a city steeped in history: in the winter of 1782, for instance, the future Czar and his wife were fêted in the theater of St. Samuel,[81] across from which, in the novel, Andreas takes his lodgings. On the other hand, however, it was a city of timeless fantasy: a "ghost upon the sands of the sea,"[82] a city of almost oriental "guile and mystery, where even walls had ears, and where every keyhole was an eye. Spies were everywhere, disguised in the cassock of an abbé or the frock of a dancer; at night the very shadows were dangerous, and there were stories of strange sacks thrown into the canal . . . or of the body of a priest found at the bottom of a well, with its skin all gone green." In short, Venice, with its Arabian Nights air of extravaganza,[83] served Hofmannsthal precisely the same purpose

---

[80] See his conversation on September 17, 1823, with the Chancellor von Müller, where he contrasts the landscape in his own novel with those in the novels of Scott.

[81] Monnier, p. 10.

[82] From Monnier's epigraph, taken from Ruskin.

[83] Monnier, pp. 5, 10.

that the exotic institution of freemasonry had served Goethe, that the oneiric *Märchenreich* of poetic vision had served Novalis, and that the "magic" mountain, some years later, would serve Thomas Mann; it functioned as a symbolic device to deepen and transcend the mundane world of the realistic novel.

Beyond the fact of its surrealistic atmosphere, Venice was suitable for another reason as well: it was the city of Casanova. Here the Faustian adventurer, the apostle of metamorphosis and the moment, could feel at home. As Monnier points out, Venice was the city of "Proteus with his sudden transformations."[84] In this "impressionistic city par excellence," as Richard Alewyn has described it, this "city of dissolving boundaries, of half-tones, of transitions between land and lagoon, between occident and orient, between Byzantine and Renaissance,"[85] Hofmannsthal's favorite type of the impressionistic, aesthetic adventurer could obviously flourish. If Thomas Mann was selecting this locale at about the same time for a novella on death, Hofmannsthal was selecting it for a novel on life for the same reason: it lies in that mysterious borderland *between* life and death, that region Rilke, in the ninth of his *Sonnets to Orpheus*, terms a *Doppelbereich*.

What does all of this, however, have to do with the Andreas of the Alpine episodes? How does the "wonderful mistress" Maria, the Venetian widow, for instance, tie in with Romana, the Austrian farm girl? The answers to such questions must begin with the fact that the Venetian events take place on a plane of reality entirely different from that of the flashback. For strangely enough, the situation is the exact reverse of what we might expect: the direct encounters in Venice are presented in a far more dream-like man-

[84] *Ibid.*, p. 190.
[85] Alewyn, *Über Hugo von Hofmannsthal*, p. 100.

ner than are the Alpine adventures, which are given through the mirror of Andreas' memory. Whereas the flashback culminates in the vision of an ultimate *Vereinigung* of the antinomies of life, for example, the Venetian episodes open with the dissociation of Maria into her other self, Mariquita; whereas the inner vision of the recollection had crystallized about the mythic unity of Gotthilff and Romana, the outer events in Venice are presented to the reader obliquely, as if through a surrealistic veil. Thus the very first paragraph, commencing as it does with a reference to a concrete time and place, dissolves immediately into a state of inward confusion on Andreas' part, occasioned by the strangeness of both the language and the situation, for the masked stranger with whom he is conversing is half-naked beneath his cloak. In fact, the entire tale of Andreas' experiences in Venice unfolds in an atmosphere of high masquerade set against a gigantic backdrop of theatrical illusion.

This highly symbolic dimension of the Venetian events—the fact that Andreas has chosen as the destination of his *Bildungsreise* a city of masks (E, 195); that he is greeted by a man in a mask; moves in next door to a theater (something he had always wanted to do [E, 120-121]); takes a room formerly inhabited by an actress; and is guided about the city by a stage designer—all of these things take on a much clearer meaning when we recall what Hofmannsthal himself was writing about the function of the theater at this time. In 1903, shortly after renouncing his private life as a lyricist for the more public role of dramatist, he composed an essay entitled "Die Bühne als Traumbild." In this he propounds what is basically a symbolist aesthetic of the stage, directed as much against the moralistic credos of a Schiller (in his "Die Bühne als eine moralische Anstalt betrachtet," for instance) as against the ideological preachments of a

178

Brecht. The theatrical mode, as is already evident in the title, is for Hofmannsthal a dream-mode; in effect, the lyrical dream of the earlier years, by virtue of being projected onto a stage, merely becomes a dramatic one. Although he would certainly agree with Schiller that the theater must foster a classical sense of community, he would obviously also support Brecht's view that the stage must reject the crude mimetic mode of naturalism: precisely *because* of its manifest relation to "reality," the theater must be doubly sure to preserve its symbolic function. In effect, then, Hofmannsthal replaces Brecht's "never-never land of the philosophical parable"[86] with the never-never land of the symbolic dream. The designer of the stage and its settings (here we think of the brilliant *Regisseur* Max Reinhardt, whom Hofmannsthal greatly admired and whose first production of a Hofmannsthal play took place that same year) must consequently be at least half poet, for he alone is responsible for the fact that the imaginary room of the stage preserve the symbolic economy of the dream (PII, 63). In short, the stage must become the infinite reflection of the finite world, a "dream of all dreams" (PII, 66, 63).

Venice, then, by virtue of its stress on masks and theater, becomes a sort of narrative dream set in the novel, a fictional stage upon which Andreas' dream-self can act out its shadowy existence. And this is precisely where Maria enters in. For much as with the *Doppelgänger* figures in the *Märchen* of Hoffmann, Maria-Mariquita is actually nothing but a symbolic projection of the psychic split in the hero himself. The two faces of the strange heroine—the excessively spiritual Maria and the irrepressibly sensuous Mariquita—are merely hypostatized forms of Andreas' own unconscious, and thus the city becomes a dream-theater of

[86] Walter Sokel's phrase, quoted by Peter Demetz, ed., *Brecht: A Collection of Critical Essays* (Englewood Cliffs, N.J., 1962), p. 7.

his inner self. This fact is suggested by several aspects of the novel. First, there is in all of the Venetian events a histrionic consciousness of both gesture and rhetoric; episodes pass in a dream-like array and with an almost obsessive attention to small physical details (often reminiscent of the dream-mode of narration in Kafka). From the masked Venetian's silent "motions and manners" as he proceeds across the stage-like piazza, Andreas recognizes that he is a nobleman even before he speaks (E, 114). Andreas' landlord, the impoverished count, speaks with both decorum and restraint: "The manner in which he had uttered these few sentences," as Andreas notes at one point, "was indeed a masterpiece of propriety and artistry," a fact even commented on by the daughter. "What do you think of the way my father expresses himself?" she asks Andreas (E, 166). Upon departing, the father lays his hand for a moment on Andreas' arm, and Andreas notices that the hand is "white and extraordinarily well-formed, but actually too small for a man and therefore unpleasant" (E, 165). Letting his hand sink "with an inimitable gesture," the father departs with a bow. Several minutes later the daughter touches Andreas' arm with "exactly the same gesture as her father had used earlier" (E, 168). Again, on meeting Sacramozo for the first time, Andreas believes that he has never before perceived a "more wonderful harmony between the bearing of a man and the tone of his voice" (E, 173). Likewise, it is the similarity in *gesture* between Maria and Mariquita that leads Andreas to guess that they are actually one and the same person: "It seemed now beyond a doubt that there had been a mysterious connection between the two gestures" (E, 184); elsewhere he even compares their hands— Mariquita's always fiery hot, Maria's always in gloves (E, 208)—and he himself at one point "blushes at an in-

180

voluntary movement of his hand" (E, 175). In sum, Venice, as the home of ballet dancers, clowns, acrobats, pantomimists, comedians, and other players, is of necessity a place where one "speaks," as Monnier puts it, with one's whole body, with hands, fingers, and gestures[87] (the language of gesture, we recall, was for Hofmannsthal the language of the whole man).

Another factor creating the surrealistic mood of the Venetian episodes and their atmosphere of dream-like projections is the fact that Andreas' quest, much like that of a Kafka hero, is apparently common knowledge before he even arrives. From every quarter he receives instructions, advice, and admonitions. Zorzi, for instance, recommends hiring men from the Rialto if Andreas gets into any trouble, and in addition offers to procure anything that Andreas might need from the theater across the canal. Andreas' new landlord greets him with the words, "You've come here to have adventures and experiences" (E, 165), while Zustina, the fifteen-year-old daughter, immediately delivers a lengthy and stilted admonishment: "If you get mixed up in disputes, misunderstandings, quarrels, and so on, get your own way. Don't let anyone, man or woman, get around you with tears. . . . You look good-natured and a good man must be warned at the first step" (E, 167-168). Furthermore, frequent (again Kafkaesque) qualifiers such as "but," "however," "probably," "very," "almost," "apparently" punctuate the narrative, distancing and estranging reality, the description of Andreas' arrival being a perfect example: "Meanwhile they had reached a *very* narrow alleyway, and stood before a *very* high house which *indeed* looked distinguished, *but quite* dilapidated" (E, 115). His first view of the landlady is of a "woman no longer young, *yet still quite* pretty" (E, 116);[88] in addition, Maria first appears to him, outside the small church, as a *"seemingly* young woman... from whose pale, *but apparently very* pretty face two dark eyes were turned toward [Andreas] with a curious and, *unless the distance deceived him*, anxious fixity" (E, 177; my italics).

Another indication of the oneiric, "projected" quality of Andreas' Venetian experiences is to be found in Hofmannsthal's use of the mirror-image. Symbolizing, as we noted earlier, dream-like transitions from one plane of time and reality to another, the mirror is used at key points in the novel where there occurs a shift from present to past, or from an outer self to a self that is totally inner. Just before Andreas is overcome, for example, by the compulsive recollection of his trip through the Alps to Venice, he crosses the room and straightens a little mirror hanging on the wall (E, 120). Maria suffers her psychological transmogrification into Mariquita also while standing before a mirror: "At one point, in front of the mirror, the lady is transformed into the malicious cocotte" (E, 206),[89] an episode apparently important enough for Hofmannsthal to record again in another note, with the very same image repeated: "Alone before her mirror at one point, the countess watches how she is transformed" (E, 233). Moreover, Sacramozo's death,

---

[88] The same technique is used by Hofmannsthal elsewhere in his works to create dream-like scenes, as for example in the *Reitergeschichte*: cf. the description of Vuic as "eine üppige, beinahe noch junge Frau" (E, 52).

[89] For the full quotation, see Hugo von Hofmannsthal, *Erzählungen und Aufsätze*, ed. Rudolf Hirsch (Frankfurt a. M., 1961), p. 142. The phrase "vor dem Spiegel" was apparently omitted in the earlier edition. As Alewyn points out, precisely the same episode is to be found in Hofmannsthal's source, *The Dissociation of a Personality* by Morton Prince (New York, 1925): "She saw herself as another person in the mirror and was frightened by the extraordinary character of the expression" (p. 361).

which he senses will lead him to another plane of reality, is portrayed in a similar fashion: "In this way his withdrawal is charming, like one who passes into the mirror to be reunited with his brother" (E, 243). Hofmannsthal's most subtle use of the image, however, is in characterizing the ambivalent, vacillating nature of his own protagonist, for we are reminded more than once that Andreas makes his home in Vienna in the Spiegelgasse (E, 125, 146).

Aside from the mirror imagery, the surrealistic progression of events, and the dream-theater background, there is yet another technique Hofmannsthal employs to create his atmosphere: the manipulation of narrative distance. Although he began the novel originally in the first person—in diary form—he soon changed to the impersonal third-person form, employing an invisible narrator with a point of view very close to that of Andreas. Not only did this form permit him to put at a distance material that was no doubt to a large extent autobiographical, but it also afforded him a far wider scope of narrative perspective and presentation. Ranging back and forth between his own point of view and that of his protagonist, he could still maintain the illusion of a single viewpoint and thus sacrifice little in structural unity.[90] During the flashback, for instance, he is quite content with keeping the two points of view fairly well separated from one another. On the one hand the narrator can comment with epic distance and objectivity on Romana: "It [the Finazzer coat of arms] is not the most beautiful, but it is her favorite" (E, 135); or on Andreas' thoughts: "The let-

[90] The same effect of two viewpoints in one (of *erlebendes* and *erzählendes Ich*, in German terms) is, of course, also inherent in a *first*-person narrative where an aging hero recounts the escapades of his youth, as for instance *Der grüne Heinrich* or *Felix Krull*. See Wayne C. Booth, *The Rhetoric of Fiction* (Chicago, 1965), pp. 286-294, and Bertil Romberg, *Studies in the Narrative Technique of the First-Person Novel* (Stockholm, 1962), particularly p. 102.

ter he wrote in his thoughts went far beyond this meager summary" (E, 145); or, in the form of more general comments, on the landscape or the weather (E, 156). On the other hand, however, usually in the more emotional moments, he assumes a position of almost direct identification with his protagonist. Such moments are often signalled by either the use of the first person: "But he [Gotthilff] wouldn't have taken that tone with the Baron von Petzenstein! It serves me right" (E, 130); or by lyrical imagery: "Romana's lips were loveliest of all: they were a clear, dark red, and shining, and her eager, innocent words issued forth from them like fiery breath from her soul" (E, 137); or even by the use of the historical present: "Andreas' throat tightens; how the fellow [Gotthilff] forgets himself and still laughs" (E, 132).

In the Venetian scenes, however, the situation is different. Here the narrator more often than not inhabits an ambiguous middle position, both on- and off-stage at the same time, and thus the reader can never be sure whether he is observing the scene through the eyes of the hero or of the narrator—whether it is merely projected or, in fact, accurately described. The narrator effectively recreates in this way the highly equivocal nature of Andreas' experiences in Venice. As in both Kafka and Hoffmann, the two authors who immediately come to mind when we read these episodes, the worlds of subject and object are strangely interwoven with one another. A prime example of this ambiguous focus of vision occurs in the scene with Nina: Andreas, while looking at her, "thought he felt how her fingers closed around his with a soft, steady pressure . . . the hint of a smile still lay on her upper lip, but it was a fading, almost anxious smile that seemed to call for a kiss" (E, 189). The elusive, dream-like air of the experience—created not only by the standpoint of the narrator, but also by the verbs "thought" and "seemed"—is in fact underscored by the narrator himself: "How," he adds, could Andreas "grasp what was so simple and so near!" (E, 190).[91] A similarly ambiguous narrative standpoint is evident in Andreas' mystifying encounters with Maria-Mariquita, particularly in the scene in the small courtyard just before he visits Nina. Before Andreas realizes what is happening, he sees two black eyes, a half-open mouth, and dark locks bearing down on him from above through a small opening: "The body lay *somehow* over the light trellis roof, the feet *perhaps* hung on a hook in the wall, the fingertips on the end of one of the posts" (E, 182; my italics). The same uncertain reality prevails in the first scene with Maria when Andreas finds her in the church. In each case, the reader must determine for himself whether the scene is real or imagined, for the narrator leaves him no hint. Furthermore, reality is estranged by the fact that all of the dialogue in Venice, in contrast to the naturalistic tone of the Alpine conversations, is highly stylized. Zustina's mode of speaking, for instance, is scarcely that of an average fifteen-year-old to her father: "But a man like you, who knows how to express himself, should be a match for anyone" (E, 163).

All of this leads us back to the question, what is the role of the enigmatic split-personality Maria-Mariquita, and how, if at all, does she relate to Romana? To answer these questions, our best recourse is to summarize an excellent article by Richard Alewyn dealing with Hofmannsthal's

[91] Fritz Martini, in his essay on *Andreas* in *Das Wagnis der Sprache* (Stuttgart, 1954), pp. 225-257, also comments on this dream-like, symbolic atmosphere of the Venetian episodes. Devoting an exhaustive *explication de texte* to a passage near the end of the fragment, Martini generally comes to conclusions less illuminating than those of Alewyn and Gautschi, although he does make the interesting observation that Hofmannsthal's narrative art situates him exactly half-way between Goethe and Kafka.

chief source for this mystifying figure in the novel, *The Dissociation of a Personality* (New York, 1906), a study by the Boston psychiatrist Morton Prince.[92] Alewyn, using the hint in the notes to the novel that "the lady and the cocotte are both Spanish; they are dissociated aspects of one and the same personality who play tricks on each other" (E, 206), demonstrates, by citing innumerable parallels, that Hofmannsthal made extensive use of Prince's study as a source for the episodes he planned about the figure of Maria. Moreover, Alewyn points out that we know from Hofmannsthal's diary (A, 157) that he had learned of Prince's work in February, 1907, and that he had immediately ordered a copy, which was later found in his library.[93] Subtitled "A Biographical Study in Abnormal Psychology," Prince's work presents the highly interesting case history of a New England college student (by the fictional name of Miss Beauchamp) suffering from multiple schizophrenia. Somewhat reminiscent of Freud's and Breuer's accounts of female hysteria, and recounted with the narrative flair of a Fielding (it culminates in a chapter entitled "The Real Miss Beauchamp at Last, and How She was Found"), the study falls into two major parts, "The Development of the Personalities" and "The Hunt for the Real Miss Beauchamp."

It is easy to see how Hofmannsthal, with his lifelong interest in the phenomena of memory, amnesia, and the dou-

---

[92] Richard Alewyn, "Andreas und die 'wunderbare Freundin'" (1955), in *Über Hugo von Hofmannsthal*, pp. 124-160. As Alewyn points out (p. 188), Prince's book later influenced a famous Irish writer as well, namely, James Joyce in his *Finnegans Wake*. In this novel, H. C. Earwicker's daughter Issy, like Maria-Mariquita, is a multiple personality based on Prince's Miss Beauchamp, and one whose mirror-selves are characteristically "yung and easily freudened" (*FW*, p. 115). See Adaline Glasheen, "*Finnegans Wake* and the Girls from Boston, Mass.," *Hudson Review*, 7 (1954), 89-96.

[93] Alewyn, *Über Hugo von Hofmannsthal*, p. 128.

ble personality, would have found Prince's work fascinating.[94] Nowhere is Prince totally unaware that in analyzing a "case" he is also necessarily telling a "history." "Aside from the psychological interest of the phenomenon" [of the dissociated personality], he writes in the introductory chapter, "the social complications and embarrassments resulting from this inconvenient mode of living would furnish a multitude of plots for the dramatist or sensational novelist," and adds that although "Miss Beauchamp is an example in actual life of the imaginative creation of Stevenson . . . I am happy to say the allegorical representation of the evil side of human nature finds no counterpart in her makeup." Miss Beauchamp, he relates, first came to him for treatment in 1898 as a twenty-three-year-old college student, and soon showed signs of undergoing a sort of multiple metamorphosis, dividing into several personalities or hypnotic selves that co-existed subconsciously and would rise alternately to the surface of her conscious self—either singly or in certain combinations. Prince is careful to add that the proper term for such a personality is neither "double" nor "multiple," but rather "dissociated" or "disintegrated," "for each

[94] See G. Wunberg, *Der frühe Hofmannsthal: Schizophrenie als dichterische Struktur* (Stuttgart, 1965). In his first chapter, "Depersonalisation und Bewusstsein," Wunberg makes the important observation that these interests were not limited to Hofmannsthal alone but also extended to the entire intellectual climate of the time, particularly in Vienna. Hermann Bahr, for instance, in his essay on Mach and "Das unrettbare Ich" (an example not given by Wunberg), makes the very Hofmannsthal-like comment: "Mich hat es sehr gequält, dies dramatisch zu fassen und einmal einen Menschen hinzustellen, der jenem anderen, der er früher war, so fremd geworden ist, dass er für Taten, die jener verübt hat, durchaus nicht mehr einstehen und Pflichten, die jener übernommen hat, nicht ohne sich, wie er jetzt geworden ist, völlig zu verleugnen, vollenden kann. Es ist mir nicht gelungen, das Problem geht wohl tiefer, als meine plastische Kraft reicht; und es ist am Ende nur an einer mythischen Gestalt darzustellen." *Dialog vom Tragischen* (Berlin, 1904), p. 96.

187

secondary personality is a part only of a normal whole self. No one secondary personality preserves the whole psychical life of the individual." These secondary personalities, he continues, had for the past six years "been playing a comedy of errors, which has been sometimes farcical and sometimes tragic. They run on and off the stage in a way confusing to the observer, changing places from moment to moment, each personating the others in scenes to which she was but a moment before a stranger."[95]

Alewyn, in his article, proceeds to show that Hofmannsthal actually modelled his Maria-Mariquita on two of the major subpersonalities of Miss Beauchamp—that of the religious saint (BI, so-called) and that of the childlike devil (BIII, or Sally). (Prince characteristically states at one point that "If this were not a serious psychological study, I might feel tempted to entitle this volume 'The Saint, the Woman, and the Devil.' ")[96] As Alewyn reconstructs the story from Hofmannsthal's notes, Maria was forced at the early age of thirteen to marry against her will (E, 205)[97] and from that time on has suffered a series of mishaps and tragedies: she loses her first child, is continually attracted to a former lover, and finally, after fighting off a fierce desire one day to see him again, she returns home to find her husband dead (E, 232-233). From this moment on, the young widow is plunged into a form of religious crisis, being consumed by feelings of unbearable guilt and by a horror of the sexual act, both of these stemming in part from her invocation of *Christ* at one point to aid her in an amorous adventure (E, 205).

All of this, however, is but a prelude to the final crisis, which, symbolically, occurs at that very moment that she sees Andreas for the first time, on his first afternoon in

[95] Prince, pp. 2, 3, 7-8.   [96] *Ibid.*, p. 16.
[97] Alewyn, *Über Hugo von Hofmannsthal*, pp. 141-142.

Venice. Dressed in a black mourning shawl and intending to pray for her deceased husband, Maria makes her way to a small church in an out-of-the-way square, where she comes across Andreas studying the church's marble façade. Passing on in silence and entering the church (precisely as Andreas, in an uncannily mirror-like scene, enters from another door), she goes to a prayer stool and kneels down. At this moment, without warning, she is transformed for the first time into her repressed alter ego: Mariquita is born. The gesture of supplication for forgiveness before the cross ambiguously dissolves into an open-armed embrace directed at Andreas, and Maria's formerly half-crippled body assumes, as if by magic, a sudden sense of childlike freedom of movement (E, 177-179). From this point on in the novel, this "wonderful mistress" functions as two entirely separate characters: the pious Maria, variously designated in the notes as Anna, the lady, the baroness, the marchioness, the countess, or merely MI or BI, and the playful Mariquita (the diminutive form of Maria), appearing as Dolores, the Spanish woman, the mask, the cocotte, the courtesan, MII, or BII.[98] Maria, being of a spiritual nature, tends towards a Christian mortification of the senses, and is only vaguely aware of her sensual and uninhibited counter-self. Mariquita, on the other hand, is well aware of her "mother-self" Maria. According to one note, in fact, Mariquita, in what could have become either a grotesque or a marvelously humorous scene, is to try to persuade Andreas to seduce Maria (E, 210).

Much mystery still surrounds the figure of Maria-Mariquita in the novel, however, and will undoubtedly continue to do so unless Hofmannsthal's *Nachlass* eventually produces more information. As it stands, the fragment actually contains only two episodes concerning Andreas and

98 *Ibid.*, p. 128.

Maria—the episode in the church and, shortly after, that in Nina's courtyard. The remainder of Maria's tale must therefore be gathered, with a great deal of patience and no final assurance of proof, from the notes, a task that, happily, has been carried out by Alewyn. (Gautschi's discussion of Maria, except for minor points, adheres basically to that of Alewyn, although here and elsewhere he quite correctly expresses reservations as to Alewyn's too-heavy reliance on Prince.) According to Alewyn, Maria will eventually be brought together with Andreas through the efforts of Sacramozo, who, renouncing his own love for Maria, will prepare them for their ultimate *Vereinigung* with each other and with their respective alter egos.[99] The union is to be crowned by an actual night of love, a fact Alewyn substantiates by a quotation from a sheet of notes left by Hofmannsthal in his edition of Prince's work: "The one who gives herself to Andreas in that night—lover, sister, mother, saint—is neither Maria nor Mariquita, but the whole woman, more than both—already belonging to God, sinning without sin—already in the world beyond."[100] From this point on, however, the ultimate shape of the novel becomes even more vague. Alewyn, for instance, assumes that Maria, now healed, will enter a convent and that Andreas will return to Vienna with Romana. Gautschi, on the other hand, sees Maria as very likely remaining in society as the countess she was before her breakdown, and Andreas as probably *never* marrying Romana.[101]

The figure of Andreas' spiritual mentor, Sacramozo, the

[99] See (E, 215, 217, 242, 244) and Alewyn, pp. 147-148.

[100] Alewyn, p. 159.

[101] Alewyn, "Nachwort" to *Andreas oder die Vereinigten* (Frankfurt a. M., 1961), p. 142, and Gautschi, p. 97; cf. also (E, 234) and (E, 220).

190

forty-year-old Maltese Knight,[102] is no less mysterious than Maria-Mariquita. Variously viewed by critics as being a fictional incarnation of Novalis, Stefan George, Rudolf Kassner, and even Hofmannsthal himself, Sacramozo is also related, in a larger sense, to the many mentor-figures who have peopled the German Bildungsroman from the time of Goethe's Abbé and Novalis' Klingsohr on down to the cluster of masters in the *Zauberberg*. As part of the Venetian configuration in general Sacramozo, like Maria, also functions to a large extent as a mirror of Andreas himself,[103] and like Maria he incorporates a striking duality: he is Christian knight and occult magician, man of the world and unworldly mystic. As Maria is mother, sister, and saint to Andreas, so the knight becomes for him a sort of spiritual brother and father. Furthermore, during that night when Andreas and Maria are finally united, Sacramozo is to commit suicide, as a symbolic gesture that Andreas has come of age and has taken over from his master (E, 217, 247).[104] This act of suicide, however, is to be understood not in a Christian sense, as a sin, but rather in a Neoplatonic sense (Sacramozo is a Neoplatonist), as a casting off of the clumsy housing of the body and as a reunion of the soul with the absolute. It is no accident that Hofmannsthal, in his notes for the knight, frequently refers to Novalis, for suicide, in the eyes of the romantic poet, was not an act of desperation, but a supremely "philosophical" act;[105] to com-

[102] Cf. (E, 217, 237). It is interesting to note that Hofmannsthal himself was forty in 1914. See Gautschi's comments, p. 75.

[103] Gautschi, pp. 65-67.

[104] Alewyn, *Über Hugo von Hofmannsthal*, pp. 146, 147-148.

[105] See (E, 217), and Gautschi, p. 79; Gautschi's entire chapter on the Knight, in fact, is excellent. It might be added here that "philosophical" suicide for Novalis could also have contained a hidden reference to his dead lover, whose name was Sophie.

mit "Selbsttötung"—absolute self-mortification or egocide—
meant for Novalis merely to pass from the confines of the
self into the infinity of the non-self, into true reality
(E, 217-218, 234). Thus, in spite of a few lingering doubts
on his part,[106] Sacramozo sees his own way as being entirely
justified; it is, indeed, *his* mode of *Vereinigung*.

What is most clear about the Venetian figures and events,
however, and what is most important from our present
point of view, is that they represent a highly ambiguous
mode of reality. The city of labyrinths is to a large degree
a stage upon which Andreas' inner fantasies are acted out:
we not only sense but also *see* the process of Bildung going
on within him. In earlier Bildungsromane, for instance, the
situation of the hero between two women was not uncommon: Heinrich Lee stands between the sensuous Judith and
the spiritual Anna, Wilhelm Meister between the philandering Philine and the good Christian Natalie. In Hofmannsthal's novel, however, given the dream-stage mode of the
Venetian happenings, the entire situation is internalized or
psychologized: Mariquita and Maria, mirror-like, dissociate
upon Andreas' arrival and reintegrate on the eve of his departure. The *Bildungsprozess* in its innermost, most private
aspects unfolds before our eyes. Aside from the dream-like
narrative elements already discussed, there is a definite hint
at this inwardness of reality by Hofmannsthal himself in the
notes to the novel. In conjunction with a projected scene of
Andreas in an "evening conversation with Zustina on the
staircase," Hofmannsthal writes that Andreas "asks her why
she did not want to get married," following this with the

---

[106] In this respect as well as in others, Sacramozo could be viewed
as reflecting Hofmannsthal's own ambivalent attitude toward Neoplatonic thought; cf. the knight's statement on death: "On dying: to
be forced to leave the theater before the curtain even went up once"
(E, 246).

note: "How could she know that he was talking about himself?" (E, 196). Moreover, there is the telling sentence at the end of the fragment itself: "This mystery [of the whole first day's events in Venice, in particular those dealing with Maria-Mariquita] was not something past, but rather something that revolved like a circle, and he had only to step back into the circle to restore it to the present" (E, 191). The experience is eternally present precisely because it lies *within* Andreas: to have it recur, he need only shift his glance to his inner self once more.

Maria-Mariquita, on one level a schizophrenic personality in her own right, is, on another, a mirror of the mythical antinomies that have plagued Andreas since his experiences at the Finazzerhof, namely, those of remembering and forgetting. These antinomies are, moreover, the same ones we discussed earlier under the rubrics of the Neoplatonic poet and the aesthetic adventurer. Mariquita, much like Hofmannsthal's other adventurer figures—like his actors and dancers—possesses a childlike attachment to the present moment and thus never experiences guilt,[107] whereas Maria, like the mythical, remembering poet in "Manche freilich," possesses a soul that is incapable of warding off even the "silent fall of distant stars" (E, 206). Like the figures of Hofmannsthal's earlier works, however, *neither* Maria nor Mariquita possesses a self: the one belongs too much to the past; the other too much to the present. Until they are reassociated with one another, however, Andreas must also remain a partial self; and until Andreas is made whole he cannot possess Romana as an inner ideal.

[107] (E, 207-209, 211, 221); cf. Alewyn, *Über Hugo von Hofmannsthal*, p. 135.

ELEVEN   Spatial Form: The Portrait of Inner Time

$\mathcal{U}$NLIKE most Bildungsromane, which attempt to present the illusion of that epic flow of time tantamount to personal growth, *Andreas* is constructed largely about a principle minimizing the sense of flux and change. As Jakob Wasserman has pointed out, everything in the novel is somehow "simultaneously there"; a "juxtaposition of weightless parts," much as in lyric poetry, characterizes the condensed style and structure of the work.[108] Gerhart Baumann, following Rudolf Kassner's insight that Hofmannsthal tended to view time spatially,[109] sees in the novel's "juxtaposition of Carinthia and Venice, of things past and things present, of waking and dream, reality and possibility" a style typical of Hofmannsthal's works in general.[110] Indeed, we need only glance at the first paragraph of *Andreas*—its juxtaposition of an outer present and an inner past—to see this same tendency at work. Moreover, unlike such Bildungsromane as *Wilhelm Meister* and the *Zauberberg*, Hofmannsthal's novel does not commence with an epic account of certain childhood *Urerlebnisse*, but rather with the compulsive recollection of much more recent events;

[108] Jakob Wasserman, "Nachwort" to *Andreas* (Berlin, 1932), p. 182.

[109] Kassner, *Die Mystik*, p. 163.

[110] Gerhart Baumann, *Rudolf Kassner, Hugo von Hofmannsthal* (Stuttgart, 1964), p. 16.

194

taken together, the eighty pages of the novel actually describe only the three days in Carinthia and part of the first day in Venice.

This temporally condensed type of narrative structure is usually referred to as being "spatial" in the sense that many pages may be devoted, not to years in the life of the hero, but perhaps to just one scene, in all of its spatial aspects. In one sense, the technique thus approaches that of the lyric, for it is capable of anatomizing, for several pages, a single object or emotion.[111] In the spatial novel it is as if—to use the analogy of the film—the epic sweep of events were suddenly run in slow motion, with the result that the spectator's attention can dwell upon the exact spatial pattern of each frame as it passes, as well as upon the relationship of the individual frames to one another. Time is not halted, but is drastically slowed, and in the process the innumerable hidden dimensions of each moment of experience, as they are projected upon the screen or the page, suddenly become apparent to the viewer. A film may take a full hour, for instance, to portray what actually occurs within the hero's mind in a span of minutes. For this reason

[111] I am referring here to what Günther Müller and other German critics have termed *Erzählzeit* and *erzählte Zeit*, and what in American criticism is known as reading-time and fable-time; see R. Wellek and A. Warren, *Theory of Literature* (New York, 1956), pp. 218-219. The latter time-span is obviously that of the fictional hero's life, whereas the former belongs to the time world of the narrator and the reader (and thus can be measured in terms of pages as well). Although these distinctions are most useful for making us aware of the narrator's role in a novel (i.e., how he weights the specific scenes in terms of the number of pages devoted to them), they can also serve as quasi-determinants for the different genres, "epic" writing expending fewer pages on longer periods of fictional time, "dramatic" writing allotting a reading-time approximately equal to the fictional time, and "lyric" writing spending several pages on brief fictional moments. Obviously, however, a single novel could easily incorporate examples of all three modes.

the technique is particularly well suited to psychological works, in which the protagonist's infinite visions and memories during one moment in life are leisurely depicted and analyzed. When the viewer leaves the theater, in other words, his own memory of the experience (memory tending to telescope events) will approach that of the hero himself.

Before pursuing the spatial form of *Andreas*, however, it will perhaps be advisable to recall very briefly the background of the term "spatial form," for much as with "myth," the concept has been somewhat blurred through overuse in criticism. The term "spatial form" was originally suggested in 1945 by Joseph Frank, who demonstrated that much of twentieth-century literature actually rejects Lessing's classical separation of genres, in particular his classification of literature as belonging strictly to the element of time.[112] On the one hand Lessing had condemned the tedious practice of giving static nature descriptions in poetry, while on the other he had rejected the perfunctory convention of painting historical allegories. Writers such as Joyce, Virginia Woolf, Proust, and Pound, in renouncing Lessing's dictum (the aesthetic of *ut musica poesis*,[113] that literature moves, like music, in time), thus returned in effect to the Horatian maxim of *ut pictura poesis*, that literature progresses, like painting, in a series of spatial snapshots or static images. Frank concluded that the chief motivation behind this trend was the attempt on the part of modern writers to thwart the flow of historical time by reaching for stabilizing, repetitive, even mythic patterns of

[112] Joseph Frank, "Spatial Form in Modern Literature," *Sewanee Review*, 53 (1945), reprinted in *The Widening Gyre* (New Brunswick, N.J., 1963).

[113] M. H. Abrams' phrase; see *The Mirror and the Lamp: Romantic Theory and the Critical Tradition* (New York, 1958), p. 88 ff.

experience; by painting scenes in prose, in other words, they partly cancelled the element of time.

Yet when speaking of this atemporal, plastic quality of modern literature, we must not forget that "spatial," much like "organic," form is not a literal but a metaphorical designation. Just as works of art do not "grow" in quite the same way that vegetables do, so novels, unlike paintings and sculptures, are neither drawn nor carved in space. The distinctions between the time-arts and the space-arts, in other words, are not as clear as Lessing would imply. This has been most simply and convincingly put by Paul Klee, who would see his own spatial art of drawing and painting, for instance, as being inseparable from the experience of passing time. "In Lessing's *Laocoön*," he writes, "a good deal of fuss is made about the difference between temporal and spatial art. But on closer scrutiny the fuss turns out to be mere learned foolishness. For space itself is a temporal concept. When a point turns into movement and line—that takes time. . . . And what about the beholder: does he finish with a work all at once?"[114] *Mutatis mutandis*, the time-art of literature—of words "moving" on a page—might be said to carry within it a spatial element as well, yet a spatiality of images that lies less on the page itself than in the memory of the reader who reads the page. T. S. Eliot, in the vocabulary of the poet-mystic, has stated the same by saying that the double quality of words—their kinship to music and time as well as to silence and space—is nothing but the relationship between movement and pattern (between reading a page, in other words, and recollecting it in the mind):

> Words move, music moves
> Only in time . . .
>
> . . . .

---

[114] Paul Klee, *The Thinking Eye: The Notebooks of Paul Klee*, trans. R. Manheim (New York, 1961), p. 78.

> . . . Only by the form, the pattern,
> Can words or music reach
> The stillness, as a Chinese jar still
> Moves perpetually in its stillness.[115]

The same idea is suggested by Thomas Mann when, in speaking of his own *Zauberberg*, he urges us to read the novel twice, stating that only in this way will we be touched by the book's timeless quality, its almost spatial aspect.[116] At first we read it, so to speak, in time, much as we might read a musical score to become acquainted with its themes; the second time, with the aid of memory, we can read it spatially as well, like a giant tapestry of interwoven motifs. Thus the timelessness experienced by Mann's hero is also reproduced in a sense, during this second reading, in the reader himself. Susanne Langer, in her theory of aesthetics, attempts to describe the same phenomenon by speaking of two "illusions," one primary, the other secondary. In painting, for example, the primary illusion would obviously be one of space, with the illusion of time remaining entirely secondary, whereas in a novel time would be of the essence and space would be subordinate.[117] Thus in *Andreas* it is precisely on this level of a *secondary* illusion that we shall discuss the quality of space. The epic flow of time is *not* halted in the novel, yet there does exist a definite tendency toward a retarding or preserving of time through a variety of formal techniques—toward helping the reader's memory, in other words, to create its spatial after-image of each scene; time "passes" in the work, but it also "accumulates."

A primary device for spatializing time in *Andreas* is the use of what might be termed literary genre painting. This

[115] T. S. Eliot, "Burnt Norton," in *The Complete Poems and Plays* (New York, 1962), p. 121.

[116] Mann, "The Making of *The Magic Mountain*," pp. 723-724.

[117] Susanne K. Langer, *Feeling and Form* (New York, 1964), pp. 117-118.

method consists primarily of portraying a scene in a particularly "fruitful" moment, one that will *suggest* action; it is most often employed in the description of scenes that present new characters for the first time. Andreas' first meal at the Finazzerhof is a perfect example. With effective use of the word "already" to halt the action, the narrator describes the scene just as if he were describing a static genre painting: "The room was handsomely arched, a huge carved crucifix on the wall. In the corner stood the table, the meal *already* served, the servants and the maids *already* spoon in hand; at the head of the table the farmer's wife, a tall woman with an honest face, yet not as handsome and cheerful as her husband, and next to her the daughter, as tall as her mother, yet still a child" (E, 131; italics mine). The description of the entire scene is essentially limited to one moment in time.

Another technique used by Hofmannsthal, and one closely related to the selection of a fruitful moment, is the device of portraiture. Again and again characters appear before the reader as mere sketches of faces and hands (much as in Hofmannsthal's "mythical" Rembrandt the light faces and hands of the portraits stand out against the dark background). Andreas' recollection of the Finazzer episode, for instance, begins with a sudden vision of Gotthilff's face (E, 122); when at the Finazzerhof, he sees Romana's mother as a face through the window (E, 138), and at the table that evening everything appears to him "as if in pieces . . . the faces and the hands" (E, 141). In Venice his first glimpse of Zustina is not of a three-dimensional figure, but of a "thin face, with dark, charmingly arched eyebrows" (E, 116), and Nina greets him as if she had just been posing for a portrait: "Everything about her was bright and of a charming, delicate plumpness. Her hair was as fair as bleached gold and she wore it unpowdered. Three things which were charmingly curved and perfectly in keeping—

her eyebrows, her mouth, and her hand—were raised to greet the guest as he entered" (E, 185). When Andreas first catches sight of Mariquita outside the church, he can discern only "one side of a pale, young face" (E, 179), much as he views it a short time later through the trellis of the small courtyard: "A human face . . . peered in. . . . Black eyes . . . a mouth half open. The pale face wild and tense . . ." (E, 181-182). The effect of this facial portraiture, with its strangely static, kaleidoscopic touch, is a retention of individual moments and separate images in the mind of the reader.

A final method of slowing the epic flow of time in the novel is that of lyric description. Not only does Hofmannsthal compress the total fictive time to that of less than a day, but he also avoids such typically epic connectives as "after" and "afterward," which would convey a sense of duration. The most frequent connectives are, instead, conjunctions expressing simultaneity (while, when, meanwhile), or adverbs of spatial immediacy (now, here, then, there). The passage of time thus becomes a series of lyric-dramatic "now"s rather than of epic "and after that"s. The scene in which Romana and Andreas visit the churchyard is a prime example of this technique: "They left the church on one side; *then* they were in the cemetery. Romana walked between the graves as if she were at home. She led Andreas to a grave; *there* several crosses stood, one behind the other. '*Here* lie my little brothers and sisters, God rest their souls,' she said and bent down and pulled up some weeds. . . . *Then* she picked up the little holy-water basin. . . . *Meanwhile* Andreas was reading the names. . . . *Then* Romana came, carrying the holy water" (E, 133-134; italics mine).[118]

[118] Dorothea Schäfer, in *Der Leserkontakt in den Erzählungen Hugo von Hofmannsthals* (Göttingen, 1962), has attempted to demonstrate that this asyndetic and deictic ("disjunctive" and continually

Time is similarly subordinated to space in the grandiose scene of the Alpine landscape at the close of the flashback. Much as in early landscape painting, each element of the scene is captured in its isolated particulars, in miniature: "*Here* a huge valley had opened, *far below* a river, no longer a mere stream, wound along, *above* it, on the other side was the mightiest peak of the range, *behind* which, the sun, still high in the sky, was sinking. Huge shadows fell upon the river valley, whole blue-black forests crowded at the broken foot of the mountain, darkening waterfalls plunged downward in the ravines; *above*, everything was free, bare, *at the very top* the snow-capped peak, ineffably radiant and pure" (E, 161; italics mine). The temporal movement in the scene—the river and the waterfall, the fast-advancing shadows and the setting sun—is framed, as it were, by static space.

Yet to determine that the underlying structural and stylistic principle of *Andreas* is a spatializing one is only the first step; the second and more interesting one is to question *why* this is the case. For by rendering entire scenes through spatial moments and lyrical imagery, Hofmannsthal creates a unique effect: together with the sense of passing time he also achieves a sense of accumulation—and in the memory of the reader as well as of Andreas. This accumulation of time is of extreme importance to Hofmannsthal's concept of the process of Bildung, which for him depends so much on an ultimate re-evaluation of past experience. Through the selection of fruitful moments and the employment of flashback and portraiture, he slows, minimizes, and conserves the flow of epic time. The theme of memory—its importance for self, morality, and Bildung—finds its stylistic analogue in the spatial form of the novel.

"pointing") style represents Hofmannsthal's effort to establish a *Leserkontakt*; this aspect appears to me much less significant than its spatializing effect.

Twelve The Novel as Unfinished Libretto

Sie sagen, wenn ich singe, mischen sich
zwei Bäche freudig, der mit goldnem Wasser,
der des Vergessens, und der silberne
der seligen Erinnerung.   (DI, 209)

OVER THE years countless theories have been advanced
as to why Hofmannsthal was never able to complete
his novel. Having begun the work when he was thirty-
three, he had completed only eighty pages of it when he
died almost a quarter of a century later. Jakob Wasserman, in his postscript to the novel's first edition in 1932,
implies that it was the tragic collapse of the Austro-
Hungarian monarchy, the Habsburg world of Hofmannsthal's youth and early manhood, that finally brought this
particular project of the poet to a standstill. C. J. Burckhardt, on the other hand, feels that it was due to Hofmannsthal's long and frustrated attempt to complete
Der Turm, the magnum opus of his later years. Karl
Gautschi, approaching the question from a more psychological viewpoint, finds, like Hermann Broch before him,
that it was the highly self-confessional nature of *Andreas*
that ultimately rendered it impossible for Hofmannsthal
to finish; the poet was, as Broch had put it, too strongly
oriented toward an aesthetic of absolute objectivity to be
able to cope effectively with the extremely autobiographical themes in the novel.

There is, however, at least one more reason why Hofmannsthal did not complete, and perhaps never could
have completed, *Andreas*. This was, briefly, the innate
difficulty of portraying Andreas' ideal love for Romana in
such a realistic form as that of the novel. Indeed, we need

202

only recall the examples of *Hyperion* and *Heinrich von Ofterdingen*, two earlier Bildungsromane with no definite ending, to realize the immense difficulty of depicting in the medium of prose the fulfillment of an ideal love. For without the aid of a formal framework of poetic meter or a thematic one of transcendence (as in Dante's case), the prophecy of paradise regained through love tends to remain a mere prophecy, an unrealized ideal. Moreover, the conclusion of the Bildungsroman is obviously more problematic than that of most novels. For if the plot closes with the classic "comic" ending of the hero's marriage, as in *Wilhelm Meister* and *Nachsommer*, this not only tends to devalue the Bildung by setting it a mundane goal, but also creates the illusion that the hero has achieved some form of permanent plateau in his development. The open ending, on the other hand (as in *Hyperion* or *Malte*), although it adheres more closely to the openness of the life-process itself, must sacrifice formal and symbolic completeness. It is impossible, in other words, for the Bildungsroman to be mimetically true to both life *and* art—to be true to the reality of unending change and growth *and* to the Aristotelian ideal of a fixed beginning, middle, and end.

However, no matter which reason or reasons lay behind Hofmannsthal's inability to finish the novel, he did provide us with a possible conclusion to it, in an entirely different art-form. For in his opera collaborations with Richard Strauss he produced libretti in which all of the major themes of *Andreas* reappear and are carried to their symbolic conclusions. With the aid of music and the operatic stage, it seems—a world where the willing suspension of disbelief was more easily achieved than in the realistic novel—Hofmannsthal was finally able to give expression to his complex ideas of an immanent-transcendent, ideal love and an allomatic constancy within change.

Three of the libretti in particular display striking parallels to the novel: *Ariadne auf Naxos* (1912), *Die Frau ohne Schatten* (1919), and *Die ägyptische Helena* (1928), all composed in the period during and after the work on *Andreas*.[119] The most obvious parallel lies in the symbolic settings of the works: just as the action of the novel takes place among the islands and lagoons of Venice, so the events in all three of the libretti also take place on islands— a sign, as in Shakespeare's *Tempest*, for example, of their highly dream-like, "operatic" atmosphere; they are clearly set apart from the world of real events. Moreover, all three libretti feature in their titles and leading roles heroines who, like Romana and the "wonderful mistress" in *Andreas*, figure in tales of allomatic transformation and ideal love. As in so many of Hofmannsthal's works, it is the female principle here that assumes the center of the stage and that provides the focal point of the final solution—much as the wise Marschallin in *Der Rosenkavalier*, for instance, functions as a sort of *dea ex machina* in the final act. For Hofmannsthal, like Goethe, saw woman as existing on a higher plane of reality than man, and her love as possessing powers of redemption; the eternal feminine, in other words, embodied precisely those open secrets of life that can be expressed only through music (PIII, 138). Central to these open secrets, as we already know, was the mythical unification of constancy and change, *Treue* and *Verwandlung*. Thus Ariadne and Zerbinetta, the Empress without a shadow and the dyer's wife, the Egyptian and the Trojan Helens, like Maria and Mariquita in the novel, bridge the mythical

---

[119] Hofmannsthal's four other libretti for Strauss—*Elektra* (1909), *Der Rosenkavalier* (1911), *Josephslegende* (1914), and *Arabella* (1929) —also display certain parallels to *Andreas* (particularly the first draft of *Arabella*, entitled *Lucidor*), but these are far less pronounced than in the above-mentioned operas. (Except for the last two, these dates and those given above are those of the first performance.)

antinomies of life, and ultimately succeed in spanning the Delphic abyss of existence.

In *Ariadne auf Naxos*, for instance, the spiritual princess and the philandering Zerbinetta are joined—again, like Maria and Mariquita—"ironically . . . through a *lack* of understanding" (PIII, 140; my italics). Ariadne is a "woman in a million, the woman who never forgets" (LIII, 29), whereas the dancer Zerbinetta, like Mariquita and the island dancers of "Furcht," is totally a creature of the moment. What in the novel is only provided for in the notes—that is, the healing of Maria's psychic wound—is actually portrayed in the opera: through Bacchus, Ariadne overcomes her memories of Theseus (as Maria is to overcome the guilt-feelings about her first husband), and at the same time is brought to the ultimate discovery of a new and deeper self. Moreover, the new self is grounded in a new awareness of vertical time, of those "immeasurable depths of our own nature, that bond between us and that ineffable, eternal element that is close to the times of our childhood" (PIII, 139).

Die Frau ohne Schatten centers upon what is merely a variation of the very same theme, only this time carried through to the problem of the unborn as well. The woman who casts no shadow, a spirit from a fairy-tale realm, is married to an earthly Emperor. Like those from the upper realm described in the poem "Manche freilich," the Empress is in desperate need of a shadow to bind her to earth; if within a year she does not provide the Emperor with a child she must return forever to the realm of the spirit, and the Emperor will be turned to stone. In the end, however, through that selfless process of self-change termed by Hofmannsthal the allomatic (in which the Mariquita-like dyer's wife is reunited with her husband as well), she is granted a shadow and with it the right to remain upon earth. The final tableau, with its background chorus of the unborn generation, presents not only a grandiose climax of the allomatic process but also an unparalleled example of the concept of vertical time; a *Vereinigung* similar to that hinted at in the title of *Andreas* here actually becomes a reality.

Die ägyptische Helena also centers on the theme of a mythical fusion of the antinomies of constancy and change —with the added parallel to *Andreas* that both the Trojan and the Egyptian Helens, like Maria and Mariquita, are actually one and the same person. In Euripides' *Helen*, upon which Hofmannsthal based his own work, there are two, however: a phantom Helen who is the cause of ten years of war and of ten thousand deaths at Troy, and the real Helen, who remains in Egypt, innocent and faithful. Menelaus, on his way home from the war with the phantom Helen, comes upon the real one in Egypt and, following various complications and subterfuges, is eventually reunited with her. To Hofmannsthal, however, this story of Helen's magical redemption from sin was artistically unconvincing. Such a plot, he argues, would make of the entire Trojan War merely a bad dream and would thus split the tale into two inorganic halves: a "ghost story and an idyll, which have nothing to do with one another" (PIV, 446). In his own libretto, then, Hofmannsthal *unites* the Helen who is guilty (who remembers) with the Helen who is innocent (who forgets). To render this paradox credible—that she can be guilty as well as innocent—he elevates her to the level of a goddess. Quoting from Bachofen's book on matriarchy ("Not for the purpose of giving herself to one man forever is Helen endowed with all the charms of Pandora"), Hofmannsthal describes his own Helen as a "strange, enchanting goddess . . . hovering above" the entire piece (PIV, 447). When Menelaus is reunited with her in the end (just as the earthly Emperor is reunited with the divine

Empress), the two Helens, like Maria-Mariquita on her night of love with Andreas, merge mystically into one. The scene is one of *Vereinigung* in its most sublime form:

> O wie du nahe,
> Unnahbare, scheinest,
> beide zu einer
> nun dich vereinest! (DIV, 300)

In a very real sense then, this closing scene of the opera, like those of the two mentioned above, represents the unwritten conclusion to the novel, a conclusion in which Andreas would finally become worthy of Romana's ideal love through the symbolic reunion of Maria and Mariquita. Just as Romana is an immanent ideal, so Helen is a wife who is also a goddess, as are both Ariadne and the Empress as well. Yet we might object at this point that the operatic world is still infinitely removed from the novelistic one, from literature in general. However, we need only listen to Hofmannsthal himself to perceive how close the two actually were. *Helena*, for instance, in the hands of an American author, would not have become a mythological opera, he comments, but rather a psychological comedy. For the occult happenings of the opera—the sudden magical remembering and forgetting on Menelaus' part—are but mythological abridgments of intricate psychological processes (PIV, 457). Without music, in other words, opera merely reverts to lyric drama—the French, Hofmannsthal reminds us, use the same word for both (PIV, 442)—and myth becomes psychology; the elves in *Helena*, for example, might become a "critique of the subconscious" (PIV, 457). Even Shakespeare's mythic dramas,[120] Hofmannsthal states, are nothing

---

[120] See Chapter 9 above for Hofmannsthal's views on myth as a general structural concept that could be applied to opera as well as to the novel, and for his specific views on the mythic dimension in the dramas of Shakespeare.

but disguised operas (PIV, 458), just as classical tragedy itself was a sung, not a spoken, art form (PIV, 442). In the end, Hofmannsthal concludes, the writer's or dramatist's techniques are very similar to those of the musician: an interweaving of analogous situations, figural similarities, and symbolic motifs (PIV, 459).

Whether or not musician and poet, tone and word, myth and psychology are actually as closely related as Hofmannsthal states is not important; nor is it necessary to argue that perhaps in opera the words are overshadowed by the music,[121] or that the success of Hofmannsthal's libretti was due precisely to the *limitations* of opera, in particular to Strauss's own "inability to cope with Hofmannsthal's psychological or metaphysical subtleties."[122] What does matter is that Hofmannsthal obviously *wanted* to believe that words and music are intimately related to one another. Just as language for him was essentially lyrical, so music was a form of meta-language, a "language," as he put it, "above all language" (PIV, 13), and just as his operas might be described as lyricized dramas, so his Bildungsroman might be viewed as narrated music. This idea becomes clearer if we recall for a moment his comments on *Wilhelm Meister*, which arose, characteristically, out of an introduction he wrote for an edition of Goethe's operas and *Singspiele*.

---

[121] See W. H. Auden, for instance, in *The Dyer's Hand and Other Essays* (New York, 1968) on the fact that in opera, "the music is so infinitely more important than the text" ("Translating Opera Libretti," p. 485); and also Susanne Langer, who states that an opera "assimilates" or "swallows" its drama much as a song does its poem (*Feeling and Form*, p. 168). "If the composition is music at all," she adds, "it is pure music, and not a hybrid of two or more arts. The *Gesamtkunstwerk*," she concludes, following an insight of Emil Staiger's, "is an impossibility" (p. 164).

[122] Hamburger, "Introduction" to the *Selected Plays and Libretti*, p. lv.

Much like Friedrich Schlegel before him,[123] Hofmannsthal finds life's "inner music" issuing from Goethe's novel at almost every point. "Mignon's funeral ceremony," he writes, actually constitutes a "complete oratorio, a religious opera without equal"; certain scenes in Book VII, he adds, are but the "musical portions" of what amounts to an *"operatic* plot" (Hofmannsthal's italics). He sums up by stating that Wilhelm's life represents a "truly ceremonial, musical idea," one that illustrates Goethe's maxim that music alone is capable of completely filling each and every moment (PIV, 178-179).[124]

In his *Buch der Freunde* Hofmannsthal makes the following note: "The present urges forms upon us. To reach beyond these and produce new forms is the creative act" (A, 51). With *Andreas,* as we have seen, Hofmannsthal was not able to do this; with his opera libretti, however, he was. Sensing, perhaps more strongly than most writers of the time, the ever-widening gap between the new awareness of psychological reality and the old modes of poetic statement, he strove to produce new forms by translating older ones into a modern idiom. Thus, by casting his most personal themes in libretto form, he succeeded in creating with Strauss what he referred to as the "truest of all forms . . . the mythological opera" (PIV, 460). Transcending with this mode his general skepticism of the word, his dislike of abstraction, and his aversion to self-confession,[125] Hofmannsthal was also able to combat what he considered the abiding evil of our time, namely the fragmentation of cul-

[123] See Friedrich Schlegel's essay "Über Goethes Meister."

[124] See Goethe's letter to Zelter, October 19, 1829.

[125] Hermann Broch, in his introduction to Hofmannsthal's *Selected Prose,* makes some interesting comments on the intimate connection between the musical mode and confessional writing (pp. xxiii-xxxiv).

ture.[126] In his eyes, the mythological opera (and with it, we might add, the social comedy) had replaced the novel as the principle vehicle of mass Bildung. With the support of music he not only could create a synthesis of all the arts, but was also able to raise the vision of twentieth-century man from the private world of the psyche to what he liked to think of as the communal theater of myth. The psycho-mythical *Vereinigung* of the title of his novel—of Andreas' divided selves with one another, of Maria with Mariquita, and of Andreas with the idealized Romana—might well have been achieved had the poet ultimately turned, as he had so many other times in the past, to music, the language above all language.

[126] See Hamburger, "Introduction" to the *Selected Plays and Libretti*, p. xv.

1874   Hugo von Hofmannsthal is born in Vienna (one year before Rilke and Thomas Mann), on February 1, the only child of Hugo and Anna von Hofmannsthal. Hofmannsthal's mother was of German descent and his father, a prominent Viennese banker, was of a family of Austro-Jewish and Italian origin.

1884–92   Attends Gymnasium in Vienna. Hofmannsthal, a lonely and precocious child, is extraordinarily gifted in languages, by the age of fifteen having read, in the original, Homer, Dante, Voltaire, and Shakespeare. He makes frequent visits with his family to the Burgtheater. At sixteen, under the pseudonym of "Loris," he publishes his first poems, and is accepted at the Café Griensteidl, the haunt of such Viennese literati as Arthur Schnitzler and Hermann Bahr. He publishes his first verse play *Gestern* the following year and also begins a problematic relationship with the German poet Stefan George, one that would last until 1906. Following graduation he takes a trip with his tutor to southern France.

1892–94   Studies law at the University of Vienna. In his first year there he publishes both *Der Tod des Tizian* and *Der Tor und der Tod* (the latter of which would become famous at Salzburg many years later), as well as his poem "Über Vergäng-

211

lichkeit," whose lines lamenting the passing of time and yet affirming the reality of the past describe those two attitudes that will most characterize his poetic thought in the years to come.

1894–95   Spends one year in volunteer service with the Imperial Dragoon Regiment in Göding (Hodonin, Czechoslovakia): from his diary, apparently a period of severe psychological depression.

1895   Upon returning to the university in October, changes from law to the study of Romance philology.

1896   Spends one month in the spring with the military, and in the summer makes his first visit to Alt-Aussee in the Alpine resort area of the Salzkammergut, east of Salzburg, where he will spend many of his future summers.

1897   Completes his dissertation on the language of the Pléiade poets. Also writes *Das kleine Welttheater*, *Der weisse Fächer*, and *Der Kaiser und die Hexe*.

1898   Spring: *Die Frau im Fenster* opens in Berlin— the first production of a play of his. After being granted his doctoral degree he spends the summer with the military and the fall in Venice.

1899   Meets Gerhart Hauptmann in Berlin in the spring. Writes *Das Bergwerk zu Falun*, the last of his lyric dramas.

1900   Springtime in Paris: meets Maeterlinck and Rodin.

1901   A turning point in Hofmannsthal's life. In June, at the age of twenty-seven, he marries the twenty-one-year-old Gertrud Schlesinger, the daughter of a banker and a girl whom he had known for six years. They settle in an eighteenth-century manor house in Rodaun, a quiet village southwest of Vienna where Hofmannsthal will spend the rest of his life, apart from summers in the Salzkammergut and frequent trips. In December he withdraws from the university, giving up the idea of becoming a professor of French to become a full-time writer; his withdrawal obviously stemmed in part from the fact that his habilitation thesis on Victor Hugo had not been accepted immediately.

1902   His daughter Christiane, who later marries the Indologist Heinrich Zimmer, is born. Hofmannsthal publishes the famous "Chandos Brief," and during the fall is in Rome and Venice.

1903   His son Franz is born. *Elektra* opens in Berlin, with staging by Max Reinhardt.

1906   His son Raimund (the third and last child) is born. He makes a lecture tour in Germany: "Der Dichter und diese Zeit."

1907   In June visits Venice; begins the novel *Andreas*. Writes the impressionistic essays "Die Wege und die Begegnungen," "Die Briefe des Zurückgekehrten," "Furcht," and "Erinnerung schöner Tage." In the fall Rilke visits him in Rodaun.

1908   Visits Greece in the spring with two friends (a trip later recorded in the travel memoir "Augenblicke in Griechenland").

1911   The opera *Der Rosenkavalier* (with music by Richard Strauss) opens in Dresden; *Jedermann* opens in Berlin.

1912–13   Renews work on *Andreas*.

1914–18   During the war years Hofmannsthal is involved in intelligence work, and is sent as an interpreter of the Austrian cause to the occupied countries of Poland and Belgium as well as to Sweden and Switzerland. Aside from his political speeches abroad, he takes an active part in the Austrian effort at home by contributing articles to newspapers and journals and by founding a multivolume cultural history of Austria, to which he contributes a study of Prince Eugene of Savoy. The downfall at the end of the war of the Habsburg monarchy signifies for Hofmannsthal the collapse of the Austro-Hungarian world of his childhood. During the war his father dies. (His mother had died in 1904.)

1919   The opera *Die Frau ohne Schatten* opens in Vienna.

1920   Together with Max Reinhardt he founds the Salzburger Festspiele, which open with *Jedermann*.

1921   *Der Schwierige*, his best-known comedy, opens in Vienna.

1922   His commonplace book or book of aphorisms, the *Buch der Freunde*, is published.

1925   Travels to Morocco in February and March, then to London and Oxford in May and June. His tragedy *Der Turm*, based on Calderón's *Life is a Dream*, appears.

214

1926   Writes prologue for Brecht's *Baal*. The film version of *Der Rosenkavalier* is premiered.

1927   Delivers lecture at the University of Munich, "Das Schrifttum als geistiger Raum der Nation." Visits Sicily in February.

1928   "Stage" version of *Der Turm* (a shorter, more tragic version of the original) opens in Munich.

1929   On July 13, his twenty-five-year-old son Franz commits suicide in Rodaun. Two days later the fifty-five-year-old Hofmannsthal, about to attend the funeral, dies from a sudden stroke; he is buried next to his son in Vienna in the Kalksburger Friedhof—at his own request in the habit of a Franciscan tertiary.

1938   The Nazis destroy Hofmannsthal's statue in Salzburg and ban his books.

1945–59 Hofmannsthal's complete works appear for the first time, in fifteen volumes, under the editorship of Herbert Steiner.

1968   The Hofmannsthal-Gesellschaft is formed, under the patronage of Hofmannsthal's friend Carl J. Burckhardt.